The Essence of Thail

Preparation Guide

Alexander Becker

TABLE OF CONTENTS

INTRODUCTION

Welcome to the Land of Smiles! Thailand, a country renowned for its captivating culture, breathtaking landscapes, and warm hospitality, is a must-visit destination for any avid traveler. Nestled in the heart of Southeast Asia, this enchanting kingdom offers a myriad of experiences that will leave you spellbound.

From the bustling streets of Bangkok, where modernity meets tradition, to the idyllic beaches and islands that dot the coastline, Thailand presents a tapestry of diverse attractions that cater to every traveler's desires. Immerse yourself in the country's rich history as you explore ancient temples, wander through vibrant markets, and indulge in mouthwatering street food that will ignite your taste buds.

For nature enthusiasts, Thailand's lush jungles, cascading waterfalls, and national parks provide an adventure-filled escape. Trek through the dense rainforests of Chiang Mai or go diving in the crystal-clear waters of the Andaman Sea, where vibrant coral reefs and exotic marine life await.

Beyond its natural and cultural wonders, Thailand offers an array of activities that cater to all interests. Join a cooking class to learn the secrets of Thai cuisine, experience the thrill of traditional Muay Thai boxing, or unwind with a traditional Thai massage, renowned for its healing properties.

In this travel guide, we will take you on a virtual journey through Thailand's most iconic destinations, provide insider tips, and help you navigate the intricacies of Thai customs and etiquette. Whether you are planning a solo adventure, a romantic getaway, or a family vacation, Thailand promises an unforgettable experience that will leave you longing to return.

So, pack your bags, prepare your taste buds for an explosion of flavors, and get ready to immerse yourself in the vibrant tapestry that is Thailand. Let us be your guide to unlocking the wonders of this captivating kingdom. Welcome to Thailand!

CHAPTER ONE

Introduction to Thailand

• *Geography and Location*

Thailand, a captivating country located in Southeast Asia, boasts a rich cultural heritage, stunning natural landscapes, and a vibrant city life. From pristine beaches and tropical islands to lush rainforests and bustling cities, Thailand offers a diverse range of experiences for travelers. In this comprehensive travel guide, we will delve into the geography and location of Thailand, providing insights into the country's regions, major cities, iconic landmarks, and natural wonders.

Overview of Thailand's Geography:

Thailand covers an area of approximately 513,120 square kilometers (198,120 square miles) and is bordered by four countries: Myanmar to the northwest, Laos to the northeast, Cambodia to the southeast, and Malaysia to the south. The country's geography can be broadly divided into four main regions:

Northern Thailand, Northeastern Thailand (Isan), Central Thailand, and Southern Thailand.

Northern Thailand:

Northern Thailand is known for its mountainous landscapes, lush valleys, and rich cultural heritage. Chiang Mai, the region's largest city, is a popular destination for its ancient temples, vibrant night markets, and traditional festivals. Other notable attractions include the Golden Triangle, where Thailand, Myanmar, and Laos converge, as well as the scenic hill tribes of Chiang Rai and the picturesque Pai district.

Northeastern Thailand (Isan):

Isan, often referred to as the heartland of Thailand, is a vast and predominantly rural region. It is famous for its ancient Khmer temples, archaeological sites, and traditional folk culture. The city of Khon Kaen serves as a gateway to Isan and offers a blend of modern amenities and cultural experiences. Travelers can explore historical sites such as Phanom Rung Historical Park and the UNESCO-listed temples of Phimai.

Central Thailand:

Central Thailand is the country's political, economic, and cultural hub. Bangkok, the capital city, is a bustling metropolis renowned for its ornate temples, bustling markets, and vibrant street life. The Chao Phraya River flows through the heart of the city, offering scenic boat tours. Ayutthaya, a UNESCO World Heritage site, showcases the remnants of an ancient capital, while the historic city of Sukhothai preserves the ruins of the first Thai kingdom.

Southern Thailand:
Southern Thailand boasts some of the world's most beautiful beaches, idyllic islands, and crystal-clear waters. Phuket, the largest island, attracts visitors with its stunning coastline, vibrant nightlife, and water sports. Krabi offers breathtaking limestone cliffs and is a gateway to the popular Phi Phi Islands. The Gulf of Thailand is home to picturesque islands like Koh Samui, Koh Phangan, and Koh Tao, known for their pristine beaches and vibrant marine life.

Natural Wonders of Thailand:
Thailand's geography is replete with natural wonders. The country is blessed with diverse ecosystems, including rainforests, national

parks, and wildlife sanctuaries. Khao Yai National Park, a UNESCO World Heritage site, offers opportunities for jungle trekking and wildlife spotting. Erawan National Park boasts seven tiers of stunning waterfalls. In the south, Marine National Parks like Similan Islands and Surin Islands provide excellent snorkeling and diving experiences.

Iconic Landmarks:
Thailand is home to numerous iconic landmarks that should not be missed. The Grand Palace and Wat Phra Kaew in Bangkok showcase stunning architecture and house the revered Emerald Buddha. The Bridge on the River Kwai, near Kanchanaburi, is a poignant reminder of World War II history. Wat Arun, the Temple of Dawn, on the banks of the Chao Phraya River, is a mesmerizing sight, particularly during sunset.

Unique Geographic Features:
Thailand's geography also presents some unique features. The Mekong River, flowing along the border with Laos, offers picturesque landscapes and opportunities for river cruises. The Floating Markets, particularly Damnoen Saduak, provide a glimpse into the traditional Thai way of life. The limestone karsts of Krabi

and Phang Nga Bay create awe-inspiring vistas, and the annual Loy Krathong festival, where floating lanterns fill the sky, is a magical experience.

Thailand's geography and location contribute to its remarkable diversity and make it a fascinating destination for travelers. From the mountains of the north to the stunning islands of the south, the country offers a multitude of experiences. Whether exploring ancient temples, trekking through rainforests, or relaxing on pristine beaches, Thailand has something to offer every type of traveler. By understanding the geography and locations of the various regions, cities, landmarks, and natural wonders, you can plan a memorable journey through the enchanting kingdom of Thailand.

•History and Culture

Thailand, also known as the "Land of Smiles," is a captivating destination that offers a fascinating blend of ancient history, vibrant cultural traditions, breathtaking natural beauty, and warm hospitality. This travel guide aims to delve into the historical and cultural highlights of Thailand, providing valuable insights and recommendations for an enriching journey through this diverse country.

I. Historical Significance:

Ancient Kingdoms:
Thailand boasts a rich historical heritage, with several ancient kingdoms shaping its past. The Sukhothai Kingdom, known for its stunning temples and Buddhist art, flourished from the 13th to the 15th centuries. Ayutthaya, the capital of the Kingdom of Siam, thrived between the 14th and 18th centuries and left behind impressive ruins, such as the Ayutthaya Historical Park.

Royal Legacy:
The Chakri Dynasty, which began in 1782, continues to reign in Thailand today. The Grand Palace in Bangkok serves as a testament to the opulence and grandeur of this era, housing the revered Emerald Buddha and other architectural marvels. Visitors can witness the intricate rituals and ceremonies

associated with the monarchy, including the Royal Barge Procession.

II. Architectural Marvels:

Temples and Wats:
Thailand is renowned for its magnificent temples, or wats, which showcase stunning architectural styles and religious significance. The Wat Arun (Temple of Dawn) in Bangkok, adorned with colorful porcelain tiles, and the Wat Phra That Doi Suthep in Chiang Mai, perched on a hilltop offering panoramic views, are must-visit landmarks. The ancient city of Sukhothai also boasts numerous temples, including Wat Mahathat and Wat Si Chum.

Grandeur of Thai Palaces:
In addition to the Grand Palace, Thailand features other majestic palaces that reflect the country's rich cultural heritage. The Bang Pa-In Summer Palace near Ayutthaya showcases a blend of Thai, European, and Chinese architectural styles, while the Vimanmek Mansion in Bangkok is the world's largest golden teak building, offering a glimpse into royal life.

III. Cultural Traditions:

Buddhism:
Buddhism is deeply ingrained in Thai culture, shaping the daily lives of its people. Temples serve as spiritual sanctuaries, and participating in a traditional almsgiving ceremony or observing monks in their saffron robes offers insight into the Buddhist way of life. Wat Phra Kaew in Bangkok houses the revered Emerald Buddha, considered Thailand's most sacred religious icon.

Festivals and Celebrations:
Thai festivals are vibrant and joyous occasions that offer a glimpse into the country's cultural tapestry. The Songkran Festival, Thailand's New Year celebration, involves exuberant water fights symbolizing the washing away of the past year's misfortunes. The Loy Krathong Festival, where thousands of beautifully decorated lanterns are released into rivers and lakes, signifies letting go of negativity and making wishes for the future.

IV. Cultural Diversity:

Hill Tribes:
Venturing into northern Thailand provides an opportunity to explore the cultural diversity of

its hill tribes. The Karen, Lisu, and Akha tribes, among others, have preserved their distinct customs, attire, and handicrafts. Visitors can engage in responsible tourism initiatives that support these communities while gaining insights into their way of life.

Thai Cuisine:
No exploration of Thai culture is complete without savoring its world-renowned cuisine. From the fiery flavors of spicy curries to the delicate balance of sweet and sour in pad Thai, Thailand's gastronomy is a delight for the senses. Exploring bustling street markets, taking a cooking class, or sampling regional specialties like Khao Soi in Chiang Mai enhances the cultural experience.

Thailand's history and culture provide an enchanting backdrop for travelers seeking an immersive and enlightening journey. From the ancient temples and ruins that tell tales of bygone eras to the vibrant festivals and diverse hill tribes that showcase the richness of Thai traditions, this captivating country never fails to leave a lasting impression. Embrace the warm hospitality, indulge in delicious cuisine, and immerse yourself in the historical and cultural wonders that Thailand has to offer.

•Climate and Best Time to Visit

Thailand, known as the "Land of Smiles," is a captivating country that offers a diverse range of experiences for travelers. From pristine beaches and lush jungles to bustling cities and ancient temples, Thailand has something for everyone. Before embarking on your Thai adventure, it is essential to understand the climate and the best time to visit to make the most of your trip. This comprehensive travel guide will provide valuable insights into Thailand's climate patterns, regional variations, and the ideal time to visit different parts of the country.

Thailand's Climate:
Thailand's climate can be classified as tropical, with high temperatures and humidity year-round. However, the country experiences three distinct seasons: the hot season, the rainy season, and the cool season. Understanding

these seasons is crucial for planning a successful trip to Thailand.

1.1 Hot Season (March to May):

The hot season in Thailand is characterized by scorching temperatures, often exceeding 35°C (95°F) in some regions. The humidity levels can also be quite high during this period. Despite the intense heat, this season attracts visitors who wish to indulge in beach activities and explore coastal areas. Islands like Phuket, Koh Samui, and Krabi offer stunning beaches and a vibrant atmosphere, making them popular tourist destinations during the hot season.

1.2 Rainy Season (June to October):

The rainy season in Thailand is marked by frequent showers and thunderstorms, particularly in the afternoons and evenings. While the rainfall can vary across different regions, the country's western coast and the Gulf of Thailand experience the heaviest downpours. Despite the rain, this season has its advantages, such as lush greenery, fewer crowds, and discounted prices on accommodation and flights. The rainforests of Khao Sok National Park and the cultural sites in Chiang Mai are excellent places to visit during this season.

1.3 Cool Season (November to February):
The cool season is the most popular time to visit Thailand due to its pleasant weather and relatively low humidity levels. Temperatures range from 20°C to 30°C (68°F to 86°F), making it ideal for outdoor activities and exploring the country's many attractions. The cool season coincides with the peak tourist season, so it is advisable to make bookings well in advance. Bangkok, Ayutthaya, and Sukhothai are some of the must-visit destinations during this time.

Regional Variations:
Thailand's climate is influenced by its diverse topography, resulting in regional variations across the country. It is important to consider these variations when planning your itinerary.
2.1 Northern Thailand:
Northern Thailand experiences milder temperatures compared to other regions. During the cool season, the nights can be chilly, so carrying a light jacket is recommended. Chiang Mai, Pai, and Mae Hong Son are popular destinations in this region, offering a mix of cultural experiences, stunning landscapes, and vibrant festivals like the Yi Peng Lantern Festival.

2.2 Central Thailand:
Central Thailand, including Bangkok, experiences similar weather patterns to the rest of the country but with slightly higher temperatures. The cool season is the most pleasant time to explore this region's historical sites, including the Grand Palace, Wat Arun, and Ayutthaya's ancient ruins.

2.3 Eastern Thailand:
Eastern Thailand, including Pattaya and Koh Chang, has a climate similar to the central region. The beaches along the eastern coastline are popular tourist spots, and the cool season is the best time to enjoy water activities and explore nearby islands.

2.4 Southern Thailand:
Southern Thailand is divided into two coasts, the Andaman Sea coast (west) and the Gulf of Thailand coast (east). The Andaman Sea coast, including Phuket, Krabi, and Phi Phi Islands, is best visited during the cool season when the sea is calm and ideal for snorkeling, diving, and island hopping. The Gulf of Thailand coast, encompassing destinations like Koh Samui, Koh Phangan, and Koh Tao, also experiences

favorable conditions during the cool season, making it perfect for beach enthusiasts.

Best Time to Visit:

Determining the best time to visit Thailand depends on personal preferences, desired activities, and the region you plan to explore. However, the cool season, spanning from November to February, is generally considered the optimal time for most travelers. The weather is pleasant, festivals abound, and it is an ideal period to explore both cultural and natural attractions across the country.

Thailand's climate is characterized by tropical conditions, with a hot season, a rainy season, and a cool season. Each season offers its own unique experiences and attractions, allowing travelers to choose the best time to visit based on their preferences. Whether you want to soak up the sun on Thailand's stunning beaches, delve into its rich cultural heritage, or explore its lush rainforests, understanding the climate and the best time to visit will ensure a memorable and enjoyable trip to the "Land of Smiles."

•Travel Tips and Etiquette

Thailand, known as the "Land of Smiles," is a captivating and culturally rich country that attracts millions of travelers each year. With its stunning beaches, vibrant cities, lush jungles, and ancient temples, Thailand offers a diverse range of experiences. To make the most of your journey and show respect for the local culture, it's essential to familiarize yourself with the country's travel tips and etiquette. This guide provides a comprehensive overview to ensure a smooth and enjoyable trip to Thailand.

Greetings and Respect:
Thais place great importance on greetings and respect. When meeting locals, a slight bow with your palms pressed together in a prayer-like gesture, known as the "wai," is customary. Addressing people using their appropriate titles, such as "khun" for adults, shows politeness. Avoid touching people's heads, as it is considered disrespectful in Thai culture.

Dress Code:
While Thailand has a tropical climate, it's important to dress modestly when visiting

temples, palaces, or any religious sites. Both men and women should cover their shoulders and wear long pants or skirts that extend below the knees. Remove your shoes before entering sacred places, and be mindful of your attire when visiting rural areas where conservative dress is expected.

Thai Cuisine and Table Manners:
Thai cuisine is renowned worldwide for its flavors and variety. When dining, it's customary to order several dishes and share them family-style. Spoon and fork are the primary utensils used, with the spoon held in the right hand and the fork used to push food onto the spoon. Avoid using chopsticks for traditional Thai dishes. Also, never place chopsticks upright in your food, as it resembles a funeral ritual.

Public Behavior:
Thai people value harmony and politeness in public spaces. Avoid public displays of affection, as it is considered inappropriate. Public criticism, especially of the monarchy or religion, is illegal and can lead to serious consequences. Stay calm and composed in all situations, as raising your voice or displaying

anger is seen as a loss of face and will not help resolve any conflicts.

Bargaining and Tipping:
Bargaining is a common practice in Thai markets and smaller shops. However, it's important to do it with respect and a friendly attitude. Start by offering a lower price and gradually negotiate with the seller until you reach a mutually acceptable price. When it comes to tipping, it is not mandatory but appreciated. Round up the bill or leave a small tip for good service at restaurants and hotels.

Temple Etiquette:
Thailand is home to magnificent temples that are revered religious sites. When visiting, ensure you are appropriately dressed and remove your shoes before entering. Avoid pointing your feet towards the Buddha images or any monks, as feet are considered the lowest part of the body. Refrain from touching or climbing on sacred objects, and maintain a respectful demeanor within the temple premises.

Local Customs and Traditions:
Thailand is rich in cultural customs and traditions. Participate respectfully in local

festivals, such as Songkran (Thai New Year), Loy Krathong (festival of lights), or the Yi Peng lantern festival. Avoid making negative comments about the monarchy or engaging in discussions about sensitive political topics, as this can offend locals.

Transportation and Safety:
Thailand has a variety of transportation options, including tuk-tuks, taxis, and buses. Ensure you negotiate the fare before boarding a tuk-tuk or taxi. Use official taxis with meters or negotiate the price in advance. When using public transportation, be cautious of your belongings, especially in crowded areas. Travel with reputable companies for long-distance journeys and follow safety guidelines while enjoying water activities or jungle treks.

Language and Communication:
While English is spoken in tourist areas, learning a few basic Thai phrases can go a long way in building connections and showing respect. Common phrases like "hello" (sawatdee), "thank you" (khob khun), and "goodbye" (laa gòn) can help you engage with locals and enhance your travel experience.

Environmental Responsibility:

Thailand is blessed with breathtaking natural beauty, and it's crucial to be a responsible traveler. Respect nature by not littering, participating in eco-friendly activities, and supporting local initiatives focused on sustainability. Avoid exploiting wildlife or supporting activities that harm animals, such as elephant riding or visiting venues promoting animal cruelty.

By following these travel tips and etiquette guidelines, you can have an enriching and respectful experience while exploring the wonders of Thailand. Show appreciation for the local customs, traditions, and people, and you will create lasting memories and leave a positive impact on the communities you visit. Embrace the warmth and hospitality of the Land of Smiles, and your journey through Thailand will be truly unforgettable.

CHAPTER TWO

Essential Travel Information

- ***Visa Requirements and Entry Regulations***

Thailand, a captivating destination known for its vibrant culture, stunning beaches, and ancient temples, welcomes millions of tourists each year. If you're planning a trip to this enchanting country, it's important to familiarize yourself with the visa requirements and entry regulations to ensure a smooth and hassle-free journey. This comprehensive Thailand travel guide provides essential information about visa types, visa-exempt countries, visa-on-arrival, and other important entry regulations to help you navigate through the process and make the most of your visit to the Land of Smiles.

Visa Types
Thailand offers several visa options tailored to meet the diverse needs of travelers.

Understanding the visa types will help you determine which one is most suitable for your purpose of visit. Here are the key visa categories:

a. Tourist Visa: The tourist visa is designed for individuals visiting Thailand for recreational or leisure purposes. It allows a stay of up to 60 days and can be extended for an additional 30 days at the Immigration Bureau in Thailand.

b. Non-Immigrant Visa: The non-immigrant visa is suitable for those planning to engage in activities such as business, employment, education, or retirement in Thailand. Various sub-categories exist, including business visa (B), education visa (ED), and retirement visa (O-A).

c. Transit Visa: If you have a layover in Thailand and will be staying for a short duration, a transit visa is required. This visa allows a stay of up to 30 days but does not permit entry into the country beyond the transit area.

Visa-Exempt Countries
Thailand has established visa exemption agreements with numerous countries, allowing their citizens to enter without a visa for a

specified period. As of the time of writing, citizens from 64 countries, including the United States, Canada, the United Kingdom, Australia, and most European nations, can enter Thailand for tourism purposes for up to 45 days without a visa. It's important to check the latest information as visa policies can change.

Visa-on-Arrival

For travelers from countries that are not eligible for visa exemption, Thailand offers a visa-on-arrival option. This allows visitors to obtain a visa upon arrival at designated ports of entry, including airports and land border checkpoints. The visa-on-arrival is valid for 15 days and can be extended once for an additional 15 days.

Visa Extension

If you wish to extend your stay in Thailand beyond the duration allowed by your visa or visa exemption, it is possible to apply for a visa extension. For example, tourist visa holders can extend their stay by an additional 30 days at the Immigration Bureau in Thailand. However, it's essential to apply for an extension before your current visa expires to avoid any penalties or immigration issues.

Entry Regulations and Requirements

To ensure a smooth entry into Thailand, it's crucial to comply with the country's entry regulations and requirements. Here are some key points to consider:

a. Passport Validity: Your passport must be valid for at least six months from the date of entry. Ensure that your passport has sufficient blank pages for immigration stamps.

b. Proof of Accommodation: It's advisable to have confirmed hotel reservations or a letter of invitation from a host in Thailand, especially when applying for a visa.

c. Return Ticket: Immigration officials may request proof of onward or return travel, demonstrating that you have plans to leave Thailand before your authorized stay expires.

d. Sufficient Funds: It is recommended to carry sufficient funds to cover your expenses during your stay. Although not always checked, having proof of financial means, such as bank statements or cash, can help facilitate the entry process.

e. Prohibited Items: Thailand has strict regulations regarding the import and export of certain items, including narcotics, firearms, and cultural artifacts. Familiarize yourself with these restrictions to avoid any legal complications.

f. COVID-19 Regulations: Due to the ongoing global pandemic, Thailand has implemented specific COVID-19 entry requirements. These may include presenting a negative PCR test, obtaining health insurance coverage, or complying with quarantine measures. Stay updated with the latest information from the Royal Thai Embassy or Consulate in your country.

Thailand's visa requirements and entry regulations are essential factors to consider when planning a visit to this captivating country. By understanding the different visa types, visa exemptions, visa-on-arrival, and complying with entry regulations, you can ensure a seamless and enjoyable journey. Remember to check the latest updates from official sources to stay informed about any changes or additional requirements. Armed with this knowledge, you can embark on your

Thai adventure with confidence, ready to explore the rich cultural heritage and natural wonders that await you in the Land of Smiles.

•Currency and Money Matters

When planning a trip to Thailand, it is essential to familiarize yourself with the country's currency and money matters to ensure a smooth and hassle-free experience. Thailand's vibrant culture, stunning landscapes, and bustling cities attract millions of visitors each year, making it crucial for travelers to have a solid understanding of the local currency, exchange rates, banking services, and money-saving tips. This comprehensive travel guide provides you with all the necessary information regarding currency and money matters in Thailand.

Currency in Thailand:

The official currency of Thailand is the Thai Baht (THB). It is denoted by the symbol "฿" and is divided into 100 Satang. Banknotes are available in denominations of 20, 50, 100, 500, and 1,000 Baht, while coins come in 1, 2, 5, and 10 Baht, as well as 25 and 50 Satang. It is advisable to carry a combination of cash and debit/credit cards during your trip.

Currency Exchange:

a. Exchanging Currency: Currency exchange services are widely available in Thailand, including at airports, hotels, local banks, and currency exchange booths. It is recommended to exchange your currency at reputable establishments to ensure fair rates and avoid scams.

b. Exchange Rates: Exchange rates fluctuate daily, and it is advisable to check rates from reliable sources such as banks or currency exchange websites to get the best value for your money.

c. Hidden Charges: Pay attention to hidden charges, such as service fees or commissions, when exchanging currency. Some places may offer no commission but provide lower exchange rates, while others may charge a commission but offer better rates.

ATMs and Banking Services:

a. ATMs: Automated Teller Machines (ATMs) are widely available in Thailand, especially in urban areas. They accept major international debit and credit cards and dispense Thai Baht. Be aware of potential fees imposed by your home bank and the local bank for using ATMs abroad.

b. Cash Withdrawal Limits: Some ATMs in Thailand have withdrawal limits per transaction, typically ranging from 10,000 to 20,000 Baht. If you require a larger amount, you may need to make multiple withdrawals or visit a bank.

c. Inform Your Bank: Before traveling to Thailand, inform your bank about your travel plans to prevent your cards from being blocked due to suspicious activities. Additionally, inquire about any international transaction fees or card usage restrictions.

Credit and Debit Cards:

a. Card Acceptance: Major credit and debit cards such as Visa, Mastercard, and American Express are widely accepted in hotels, restaurants, shopping malls, and tourist attractions. However, it is always wise to carry some cash, especially in smaller establishments or remote areas where card acceptance may be limited.

b. Dynamic Currency Conversion: When using your card for transactions, be cautious about dynamic currency conversion. This allows merchants to convert the transaction amount into your home currency, but the conversion rate may be unfavorable. Opt to pay in Thai Baht instead.

Traveler's Checks:

While traveler's checks were once popular, their usage has significantly declined in Thailand. Many businesses and banks no longer accept them, and the exchange rates offered may be less favorable than for cash. It is recommended to use cash or cards instead.

Money-Saving Tips:

a. Bargaining: Bargaining is common in Thai markets and street stalls. Practice your negotiation skills to secure better prices, but be respectful and maintain a friendly attitude.

b. Tipping: Tipping is not obligatory in Thailand, but it is appreciated for exceptional service. Leave a small amount of change or round up the bill in restaurants and consider tipping tour guides and drivers.

c. Local Food and Street Eateries: Enjoying local street food is not only a delicious experience but also a budget-friendly option. Thailand is renowned for its culinary delights, and sampling street food is a must-do for any visitor.

d. Transportation: Utilize affordable transportation options such as tuk-tuks, public buses, or the BTS Skytrain in Bangkok to save money on commuting.

e. Local Markets: Explore local markets for inexpensive clothing, souvenirs, and unique handicrafts. These markets offer a vibrant atmosphere and an opportunity to immerse yourself in Thai culture.

Understanding the currency and money matters in Thailand is crucial for a smooth and enjoyable travel experience. By familiarizing yourself with the Thai Baht, currency exchange options, banking services, and money-saving tips, you can make the most of your trip while managing your finances effectively. Remember to stay vigilant, use reputable sources for currency exchange, and notify your bank about your travel plans. With this comprehensive travel guide, you can confidently navigate the financial aspects of your Thailand adventure and focus on creating unforgettable memories.

• *Language and Communication*

Thailand, known for its vibrant culture, stunning landscapes, and warm hospitality, attracts millions of visitors each year. While exploring this enchanting country, it's essential to understand the nuances of language and communication to fully immerse oneself in Thai society. In this travel guide, we will delve into the rich linguistic landscape of Thailand, discuss the primary language spoken, explore regional variations, highlight useful phrases for travelers, and touch upon non-verbal communication customs. Let's embark on a linguistic journey through the Land of Smiles!

The Thai Language:

Thai, the official language of Thailand, is spoken by the majority of the population. It belongs to the Tai-Kadai language family and has its roots in an ancient script called "Khmer." Thai is a tonal language with five distinct tones, making it a fascinating linguistic experience for visitors. Learning a few basic phrases will not only enhance your travel experience but also demonstrate your respect for Thai culture.

Useful Phrases for Travelers:

To facilitate communication, here are some essential Thai phrases and expressions that every traveler should know:

a) Greetings and Politeness:

"Sawasdee" - Hello/Goodbye
"Khop khun" - Thank you
"Khor thot" - Sorry/Excuse me
b) Basic Questions:

"Sabai dee mai?" - How are you?
"Hong naam yoo tee nai?" - Where is the restroom?
"Nee tao rai?" - How much is this?
c) Ordering Food:

"Khor chue-ay" - Please give me...
"A-harn" - Food
"Nam pla" - Fish sauce (common condiment)
d) Emergency Phrases:

"Chuay duay" - Help!
"Rong-rian yuu nai?" - Where is the nearest hospital?
"Phom yak tong kan" - I need to make a phone call.
Regional Language Variations:

Thailand's linguistic diversity extends beyond the official language, with various regional dialects and minority languages being spoken. Some notable regional variations include:

a) Isaan/Lao: In northeastern Thailand, the Isaan dialect, influenced by Lao, is prevalent. Travelers exploring this region may encounter distinct vocabulary and pronunciation patterns.

b) Southern Thai: In the south, a dialect with influences from Malay and Khmer is spoken. Visitors to the popular destinations of Phuket, Krabi, and Pattani might encounter these unique linguistic features.

c) Hill Tribe Languages: Thailand's northern region is home to several hill tribes, each with its own language or dialect. While English is commonly spoken in tourist areas, learning a few basic phrases in hill tribe languages, such as Karen or Akha, can foster deeper connections with local communities.

Non-Verbal Communication:
In Thai culture, non-verbal communication plays a significant role in daily interactions.

Understanding these customs can help travelers navigate social situations effectively:

a) Wai: The traditional Thai greeting, known as "wai," involves placing your palms together at chest level and bowing slightly. It is customary to return a wai when receiving one.

b) Body Language: Thai people value politeness and saving face. Maintaining a calm demeanor, avoiding aggressive gestures, and refraining from public displays of affection are essential for respecting local customs.

c) Removing Shoes: When entering someone's home, a temple, or certain establishments, it is customary to remove your shoes as a sign of respect.

Language Resources for Travelers:
Numerous resources can aid travelers in learning Thai or improving their language skills during their visit:

a) Phrasebooks and Language Apps: Compact phrasebooks or mobile language apps like "Learn Thai" or "Speak Thai" offer practical vocabulary and pronunciation guides.

b) Language Classes: Enrolling in a short-term language course, either online or in person, can provide a more in-depth understanding of the Thai language and its nuances.

c) Language Exchange Programs: Connecting with locals through language exchange platforms allows travelers to practice Thai while helping locals practice English or other languages.

Language and communication are vital aspects of any travel experience, and Thailand is no exception. Familiarizing yourself with the Thai language, regional variations, and non-verbal communication customs will not only make your journey more enjoyable but also enable you to connect with locals on a deeper level. Remember, a simple "sawasdee" and a warm smile can go a long way in the Land of Smiles. So embrace the linguistic adventure and create lasting memories in the enchanting kingdom of Thailand!

•Health and Safety Tips

Thailand, known for its vibrant culture, beautiful landscapes, and warm hospitality, attracts millions of tourists every year. While exploring the enchanting temples, enjoying the bustling markets, and indulging in delicious street food, it is essential to prioritize your health and safety. This comprehensive guide provides valuable tips and insights to ensure a safe and enjoyable trip to Thailand.

Travel Insurance:

Before embarking on your journey, it is crucial to have comprehensive travel insurance that covers medical emergencies, trip cancellations, and lost belongings. Medical expenses can be high in Thailand, so having adequate coverage will provide you with peace of mind throughout your trip.

Vaccinations:

Consult with your healthcare provider or a travel health clinic at least six weeks before your trip to ensure you are up to date on routine vaccinations. Additionally, consider vaccinations for diseases such as Hepatitis A and B, typhoid, and Japanese encephalitis, which may be recommended depending on the duration and nature of your stay.

Safe Food and Water:
Thailand is renowned for its delicious cuisine, but it is essential to be cautious about the food and water you consume. To minimize the risk of foodborne illnesses:

a. Drink bottled water or purified water and avoid consuming tap water.
b. Use bottled water for brushing your teeth.
c. Be cautious of ice cubes and only consume those made from purified water.
d. Eat hot, freshly cooked food from reputable establishments.
e. Avoid raw or undercooked food, including seafood, meat, and eggs.
f. Wash fruits and vegetables thoroughly or opt for peeled fruits.

Mosquito-borne Diseases:
Thailand is home to mosquitoes that can transmit diseases such as dengue fever, Zika virus, and malaria. Protect yourself by:
a. Using mosquito repellents containing DEET on exposed skin.
b. Wearing long-sleeved shirts, long pants, and socks, especially during dawn and dusk when mosquitoes are most active.

c. Sleeping in accommodations with air conditioning or screened windows.

d. Using mosquito nets if you are staying in more rustic accommodations or in rural areas.

Sun Protection:
Thailand's tropical climate means abundant sunshine, making sun protection vital. Protect yourself from harmful UV rays by:

a. Using sunscreen with a high SPF and reapplying it frequently, especially after swimming or excessive sweating.

b. Wearing a hat, sunglasses, and lightweight, long-sleeved clothing to shield yourself from the sun.

c. Seeking shade during the hottest hours of the day to prevent heatstroke and sunburn.

Hygiene and Sanitation:
Maintaining good hygiene practices can help prevent illness while traveling. Remember to:

a. Wash your hands regularly with soap and clean water, especially before eating or after using the restroom.

b. Carry hand sanitizer with you for situations where soap and water are not available.

c. Pack personal hygiene items such as toilet paper, wet wipes, and hand sanitizing gel for public restrooms or rural areas.

Traffic and Road Safety:

Thailand's traffic can be chaotic, and road accidents are common. Follow these safety guidelines:

a. Exercise caution when crossing roads and use designated pedestrian crossings whenever possible.

b. Be vigilant when using public transportation, including motorcycles and tuk-tuks, and ensure the driver adheres to safety regulations.

c. Avoid renting motorcycles unless you are an experienced rider, as road conditions and traffic can be challenging for beginners.

d. Always wear a helmet when riding a motorcycle or participating in adventure activities like zip-lining or ATV riding.

Natural Hazards:

Thailand is prone to natural hazards, including tropical storms, flooding, and earthquakes. Stay informed about the weather conditions and follow instructions from local authorities. Additional precautions include:

a. Checking weather forecasts before embarking on outdoor activities, especially during monsoon seasons.

b. Avoiding swimming in unfamiliar or unmarked waters to prevent drowning or encountering dangerous marine life.

c. Adhering to safety instructions when visiting national parks, waterfalls, or caves.

Local Laws and Customs:

Respect for local laws, customs, and traditions is essential when visiting Thailand. Familiarize yourself with the following:

a. Dress modestly when visiting temples and religious sites, covering shoulders and knees.

b. Show respect for the monarchy and avoid any disrespectful actions or comments.

c. Refrain from engaging in illegal activities, including drug use and possession.

d. Be cautious of scams and avoid interactions with suspicious individuals offering unsolicited assistance.

Thailand offers a remarkable travel experience, but it is crucial to prioritize your health and safety during your stay. By following these health and safety tips, you can minimize potential risks and ensure a memorable and worry-free trip. Remember to stay informed, plan ahead, and exercise caution, allowing you to fully enjoy the wonders of this captivating country.

• *Transportation in Thailand*

Thailand, known as the "Land of Smiles," is a captivating destination that offers a rich cultural heritage, breathtaking landscapes, and an abundance of experiences. When it comes to transportation, Thailand boasts a diverse range of options that make exploring the country a breeze. From modern infrastructure to traditional modes of transport, this travel guide will provide you with an in-depth overview of transportation in Thailand, ensuring you have a seamless and unforgettable journey.

Air Travel:
Thailand is well-connected to the world through its numerous international airports, with Suvarnabhumi Airport in Bangkok being the main gateway. Several domestic airports are scattered across the country, making air travel a convenient choice for long-distance journeys within Thailand. Airlines such as Thai Airways, Bangkok Airways, and AirAsia offer a

wide range of domestic flights, ensuring quick and efficient travel between major cities and popular tourist destinations.

Railways:
Thailand's railway network is an excellent way to experience the scenic beauty of the country. The State Railway of Thailand operates an extensive network that connects major cities and regions, including the iconic Northern Line, which winds through the picturesque countryside. The overnight sleeper trains, such as the popular Bangkok-Chiang Mai route, offer a unique and comfortable travel experience. For shorter distances, commuter trains and the Bangkok Skytrain (BTS) provide efficient transportation within the city.

Road Travel:
Thailand's road network is well-developed, making road travel a convenient option for both short and long distances. The national highways connect major cities and regions, offering easy access to various attractions. For independent exploration, renting a car or motorcycle is a popular choice, although it's important to familiarize yourself with local driving regulations. Alternatively, travelers can opt for buses, which are widely available,

affordable, and connect even remote areas. VIP buses and minivans provide more comfort and speed for longer journeys.

Waterways:

Thailand's extensive network of rivers and canals makes water travel an enchanting way to explore certain regions. The Chao Phraya River in Bangkok is a prominent waterway, with numerous river taxis and ferries shuttling locals and tourists alike. In cities like Ayutthaya and Chiang Mai, boat tours offer a unique perspective of historical sites and cultural landmarks. For longer journeys, ferries and speedboats connect popular islands in the Gulf of Thailand and the Andaman Sea, such as Koh Samui, Phuket, and Krabi.

Tuk-tuks and Motorcycles:

Tuk-tuks, the iconic three-wheeled vehicles, are an integral part of Thailand's transportation landscape. Found in abundance throughout cities and towns, tuk-tuks offer a fun and adventurous way to get around, particularly for short distances. Bargaining for fares is customary, so remember to negotiate before hopping aboard. Motorcycles and scooters are also prevalent in Thailand, offering freedom and flexibility, especially in more rural areas.

However, caution must be exercised, and proper safety gear should be worn at all times.

Mass Transit Systems:

Thailand's major cities boast efficient and modern mass transit systems that alleviate traffic congestion and provide hassle-free transportation. Bangkok's Mass Rapid Transit (MRT) and the BTS Skytrain network cover extensive areas, connecting key tourist destinations, shopping centers, and residential areas. Similarly, the Rapid Transit System (BRT) in Bangkok and the Bus Rapid Transit (BRT) in Chiang Mai offer cost-effective and reliable transportation options.

Ride-hailing Services:

Popular ride-hailing services like Grab and Gojek are widely available in Thailand, providing a convenient alternative to traditional taxis. These services can be accessed through smartphone applications, allowing you to easily book a car or motorcycle taxi, calculate fares in advance, and enjoy cashless transactions. It's advisable to have a local SIM card or access to Wi-Fi to use these services seamlessly.

Local Transportation:

Within cities, local transportation options include buses, songthaews (shared taxis or trucks with benches), and motorbike taxis. These modes of transport are not only affordable but also provide an authentic glimpse into the daily life of locals. Songthaews are particularly popular in northern Thailand and are an excellent way to explore the countryside and visit neighboring towns and villages.

Transportation in Thailand offers a wide range of options to suit every traveler's needs. Whether you prefer the comfort of air travel, the charm of rail journeys, or the flexibility of road trips, Thailand has it all. From bustling metropolises to tranquil islands, the country's well-connected transportation infrastructure ensures that you can explore its diverse attractions with ease. Embrace the various modes of transport, immerse yourself in the vibrant culture, and get ready for an unforgettable journey through the Land of Smiles.

CHAPTER THREE

Top Tourist Destinations

• *Bangkok*

As the capital and largest city of Thailand, Bangkok stands out as a bustling metropolis that seamlessly blends tradition and modernity. With its rich history, vibrant culture, magnificent temples, and vibrant street life, Bangkok has rightfully earned its reputation as one of the world's top tourist destinations. This Thailand travel guide will delve into the many facets of Bangkok, providing you with an in-depth look at the city's attractions, cuisine, shopping, and nightlife, ensuring you make the most of your visit.

Historical and Cultural Significance:
Bangkok boasts a fascinating history that dates back centuries. A visit to the magnificent Grand

Palace, home to the revered Wat Phra Kaew (Temple of the Emerald Buddha), offers a glimpse into Thailand's royal heritage. The temple's intricate architecture and exquisite details are truly awe-inspiring. Wat Arun, known as the Temple of Dawn, is another iconic landmark that should not be missed, particularly during sunset when its spires are bathed in a golden glow.

Sacred Temples and Spiritual Retreats:
Thailand is known as the Land of a Thousand Temples, and Bangkok is no exception. Wat Pho, famous for its enormous reclining Buddha statue, is not only a place of worship but also an esteemed center for traditional Thai massage and medicine. The serene atmosphere of Wat Saket, also known as the Golden Mount, offers panoramic views of the city, making it an ideal spot for introspection and reflection.

Floating Markets and Culinary Delights:
No visit to Bangkok is complete without experiencing its vibrant street food scene and floating markets. The floating markets, such as Damnoen Saduak and Amphawa, provide an immersive cultural experience where you can sample an array of delectable dishes and

interact with local vendors. From the iconic Pad Thai to flavorful green curry, Bangkok's culinary offerings are bound to tantalize your taste buds.

Shopper's Paradise:
Bangkok is a shopaholic's paradise, catering to every budget and taste. The city is renowned for its sprawling markets, including the Chatuchak Weekend Market, where you can find everything from clothing and accessories to handicrafts and antiques. For a more upscale experience, visit luxury shopping malls like Siam Paragon and CentralWorld, housing international brands and designer boutiques.

Chao Phraya River and Canal Tours:
Exploring Bangkok's waterways is a unique way to witness the city's charm. A boat tour along the Chao Phraya River allows you to admire the cityscape, passing by iconic landmarks like the Temple of Dawn and the Royal Barges Museum. Venturing into the city's intricate canal system, known as khlongs, offers a glimpse into local life and the traditional stilt houses that line the waterways.

Art and Culture:

Bangkok's art and cultural scene have been flourishing in recent years. The Bangkok Art and Culture Centre (BACC) showcases contemporary art exhibitions, while the Jim Thompson House Museum provides insight into Thai silk and traditional architecture. Additionally, the annual Bangkok International Film Festival and Thailand Cultural Music Festival attract artists and performers from around the world.

Nightlife and Entertainment:

When the sun sets, Bangkok comes alive with its vibrant nightlife. The city offers a myriad of entertainment options, from rooftop bars that provide stunning views of the city skyline to lively nightclubs and cultural shows, such as the renowned Calypso Cabaret. Khao San Road, popular among backpackers, offers a lively atmosphere with its street vendors, bars, and clubs.

Day Trips from Bangkok:

While Bangkok itself has a plethora of attractions, the city's strategic location makes it an excellent base for day trips to nearby destinations. Ayutthaya, a UNESCO World Heritage Site, showcases the ruins of an ancient capital and offers a glimpse into

Thailand's historical past. The floating markets of Damnoen Saduak and the ancient city of Sukhothai are also within reach, allowing visitors to experience the diversity of Thailand's cultural heritage.

Bangkok's unique blend of history, culture, and vibrant energy make it a top tourist destination in Thailand. Whether you're seeking spiritual enlightenment, exploring ancient temples, indulging in delicious street food, or immersing yourself in the city's thriving art scene, Bangkok has something to offer everyone. With its warm hospitality, fascinating attractions, and diverse experiences, a visit to Bangkok is sure to leave a lasting impression and create memories to treasure for a lifetime.

Wat Arun

Thailand, renowned for its rich cultural heritage and vibrant tourist attractions, offers visitors a plethora of stunning destinations to explore. Among these, Wat Arun stands tall as a must-visit site, captivating tourists with its grandeur and historical significance. This comprehensive travel guide aims to provide an in-depth look at Wat Arun, including its history, architectural marvels, cultural significance, and practical tips for visitors. Whether you are a history enthusiast, an architecture lover, or simply seeking a memorable experience in Thailand, Wat Arun promises to leave you awe-inspired.

I. Historical Background :

Wat Arun, also known as the Temple of Dawn, is an iconic Buddhist temple located on the western bank of the Chao Phraya River in Bangkok, Thailand. The temple dates back to the Ayutthaya period and has witnessed numerous historical events throughout its existence. Legend has it that King Taksin, after the fall of Ayutthaya, arrived at this spot during dawn and named the temple after the Hindu god Aruna, symbolizing the rising sun.

II. Architectural Marvels :

Wat Arun's unique architecture and intricate design are among its most captivating features. The temple's central structure, known as a prang, stands at an impressive height of over 70 meters, adorned with colorful porcelain tiles and seashells. As visitors ascend the steep stairs, they are rewarded with breathtaking panoramic views of the Chao Phraya River and the surrounding cityscape.

The prang itself embodies a blend of Khmer and Thai architectural styles, displaying intricate carvings depicting mythological creatures and religious motifs. The central prang is surrounded by four smaller satellite prangs, each representing the mythical Mount Meru, the abode of the gods in Hindu cosmology. The temple's exterior is further adorned with sculptures, stucco reliefs, and ornate spires that glimmer in the sunlight.

III. Cultural Significance :
Wat Arun holds immense cultural significance in Thai society. It is an active place of worship, attracting devout Buddhists who come to pay their respects and participate in religious ceremonies. Visitors can witness locals making merit, lighting incense, and offering prayers, providing a glimpse into the spiritual traditions of Thailand.

Furthermore, Wat Arun is an integral part of Thai festivals and celebrations, particularly during Songkran (Thai New Year) and Loy Krathong (Festival of Lights). During these events, the temple becomes a hub of vibrant activities, including traditional performances, processions, and spectacular firework displays.

IV. Exploring Wat Arun :

Temple Grounds:
Upon entering the temple grounds, visitors are greeted by a serene ambiance and meticulously maintained gardens. The pathways are lined with statues of Chinese soldiers and mythical creatures, adding to the temple's mystical charm.

Prang and Terraces:
Climbing the prang is a highlight for many visitors, but it requires caution and physical fitness due to the steep stairs. The terraces offer platforms for panoramic views and the opportunity to admire the architectural details up close.

Ordination Hall:
Located behind the prang, the Ordination Hall houses a principal Buddha image known as the Emerald Buddha. Although smaller in size compared to its famous counterpart in the Grand Palace, it holds great religious significance.

Museum and Exhibitions:
Wat Arun also houses a museum where visitors can delve into the temple's history, its restoration projects, and explore artifacts and ancient relics. The exhibits provide valuable insights into Thailand's cultural heritage and the temple's evolution.

River Cruise:
To enhance the Wat Arun experience, visitors can take a river cruise along the Chao Phraya River. This allows for a picturesque view of the temple from the water, especially during sunset when the temple illuminates, creating a magical ambiance.

V. Practical Information and Tips :

Opening Hours and Admission:
Wat Arun is open daily from early morning until late afternoon. Admission fees are nominal, and it is advisable to check the latest timings before planning your visit.

Dress Code and Etiquette:
As a place of worship, visitors are expected to dress modestly. It is recommended to wear clothing that covers the shoulders, knees, and

avoid revealing attire. Removing shoes before entering certain areas is customary.

Accessibility:
While the temple grounds are accessible to most visitors, ascending the prang may be challenging for individuals with mobility issues. However, the lower terraces still offer stunning views and a chance to appreciate the temple's beauty.

Nearby Attractions:
Wat Arun's location makes it convenient to explore other notable attractions in Bangkok, such as the Grand Palace, Wat Phra Kaew, and Wat Pho. Consider combining visits to maximize your time in the area.

Wat Arun, with its awe-inspiring architecture, rich history, and cultural significance, remains a top tourist destination in Thailand. Whether marveling at its towering prang, experiencing traditional rituals, or immersing oneself in Thai spirituality, a visit to Wat Arun promises a memorable journey. As you explore Thailand's vibrant capital city, be sure to include this majestic temple on your itinerary and allow its beauty to transport you to a realm where history and spirituality intertwine.

Chatuchak Weekend Market

Thailand is renowned for its vibrant culture, stunning landscapes, and warm hospitality. Among the numerous attractions that draw travelers to this Southeast Asian gem, Chatuchak Weekend Market stands out as one of the top tourist destinations. Located in the heart of Bangkok, this sprawling market offers an unforgettable shopping experience that immerses visitors in the local culture. In this Thailand travel guide, we will delve into the fascinating world of Chatuchak Weekend Market, highlighting its historical significance, unique features, shopping opportunities, and tips for an unforgettable visit.

I. Historical Significance:

Chatuchak Weekend Market traces its origins back to the mid-20th century when it was established as a small market catering primarily to local residents. Over the years, its popularity grew exponentially, attracting both domestic and international visitors. Today, it is one of the largest weekend markets in the world and a symbol of Bangkok's bustling street life.

II. Location and Access:

Situated in the northern part of Bangkok, Chatuchak Weekend Market is easily accessible by public transportation. Travelers can take the BTS Skytrain to Mo Chit station or the MRT subway to Chatuchak Park station. The market is adjacent to these stations, making it convenient for visitors to reach. The market is open on Saturdays and Sundays, from early morning until late evening, allowing ample time for exploration.

III. The Maze of Shopping:

Spread over an impressive 27 acres, Chatuchak Weekend Market boasts more than 15,000 stalls, organized into 27 sections. Each section offers an array of products, ranging from clothing and accessories to handicrafts, antiques, plants, and much more. Navigating the market can be an adventure in itself, as it is easy to get lost amidst the maze of narrow alleyways and bustling shops. However, this adds to the charm and excitement of the experience.

IV. Shopper's Paradise:

Chatuchak Weekend Market is a shopaholic's dream come true. The market caters to every taste and budget, with a vast selection of goods available at reasonable prices. From trendy fashion items to traditional Thai handicrafts, visitors can find an extensive range of products that reflect the country's rich cultural heritage. It is advisable to arrive with a shopping list, as the sheer variety of items can be overwhelming.

V. Cultural Extravaganza:

Beyond the shopping delights, Chatuchak Weekend Market offers a captivating glimpse into Thai culture. Amidst the stalls, visitors can savor local street food, sample exotic fruits, and indulge in traditional Thai snacks. The market is also a hub for local artists, with various art galleries showcasing contemporary Thai artwork. Additionally, live performances, including traditional music and dance, create a vibrant and festive atmosphere.

VI. Tips for an Unforgettable Visit:

Arrive Early: Chatuchak Weekend Market gets crowded as the day progresses, so it is advisable to arrive early to beat the crowds and have a more relaxed shopping experience.

Wear Comfortable Clothing: Given the size of the market and the tropical climate, it is essential to wear comfortable clothing and shoes. Sunscreen and a hat are also recommended to protect against the sun.

Bargaining Skills: Bargaining is a common practice in Thai markets, including Chatuchak. Haggling over prices can be an exciting part of the shopping experience, but it is important to be polite and respectful during negotiations.

Hydration and Snacks: With so much to explore, it is crucial to stay hydrated. There are numerous food stalls and vendors selling refreshing drinks and tasty snacks throughout the market.

Payment Options: While many stalls accept cash, some vendors also accept credit cards or mobile payment methods. It is advisable to carry a mix of cash and cards for convenience.

Map and Sections: Grab a map of the market at the entrance to help navigate through the various sections and locate specific areas of interest.

Chatuchak Weekend Market in Bangkok stands as a top tourist destination in Thailand, offering a unique blend of shopping, cultural immersion, and sensory delights. Its historical significance, expansive size, and diverse range of products make it a must-visit for travelers seeking an authentic Thai experience. As you plan your trip to Thailand, make sure to include Chatuchak Weekend Market in your itinerary for an unforgettable shopping extravaganza and an opportunity to immerse yourself in the vibrant local culture.

Floating Markets

Thailand, renowned for its vibrant culture, stunning landscapes, and mouthwatering cuisine, offers travelers an abundance of unique experiences. Among the country's most captivating attractions are its floating markets, which have long been regarded as top tourist destinations. These bustling markets, situated along tranquil waterways, provide visitors with an authentic glimpse into Thailand's rich trading heritage, offering an array of exotic products, delectable street food, and a vibrant atmosphere. In this comprehensive Thailand travel guide, we delve into the enchanting world of floating markets, highlighting their historical significance, the must-visit markets across the country, and the immersive experiences they offer to travelers.

I. Historical Significance

Floating markets have a storied history in Thailand, dating back to the time when rivers and canals were the primary modes of transportation and trade. Thailand's fertile waterways have always played a crucial role in the country's economy, and floating markets emerged as vital hubs for commerce, where villagers and traders would converge to exchange goods, produce, and crafts. These markets served as social and economic centers, fostering community ties and cultural exchange. Today, while modern infrastructure has transformed Thailand's trading landscape, floating markets continue to thrive, preserving the essence of this bygone era.

II. Top Floating Markets in Thailand

Damnoen Saduak Floating Market:

Located just a short drive from Bangkok, Damnoen Saduak is the most famous floating market in Thailand.
With its vibrant atmosphere and bustling activity, it offers a visual spectacle with vendors skillfully maneuvering their boats through narrow canals.
Visitors can explore the market by longtail boat, sampling an array of delicious Thai dishes and purchasing local handicrafts and fresh produce.
Amphawa Floating Market:

Situated in the quaint town of Amphawa, this market is renowned for its charming wooden houses and a serene canal setting.
The market primarily operates on weekends, attracting both locals and tourists.

In addition to shopping for local products, visitors can embark on a magical evening boat tour to witness the enchanting sight of fireflies lighting up the riverside.
Taling Chan Floating Market:

Located on the outskirts of Bangkok, Taling Chan offers a more intimate and authentic floating market experience.
This market emphasizes its culinary offerings, with vendors serving up an enticing array of seafood and traditional Thai dishes.
Visitors can enjoy a relaxing boat ride, explore the adjacent orchid farm, or even take part in traditional Thai cooking classes.
Bang Nam Pheung Floating Market:

Nestled in the lush greenery of Bang Krachao, often referred to as Bangkok's "Green Lung," this market offers a tranquil escape from the bustling city.
It features an eco-friendly approach, showcasing organic produce, handmade crafts, and local delicacies.
Visitors can rent bicycles to explore the surrounding nature trails, visit nearby temples, and savor the market's unique offerings.
Khlong Lat Mayom Floating Market:

Situated on the outskirts of Bangkok, this market offers a more laid-back and authentic experience.

It is known for its extensive variety of fresh fruits, vegetables, and ready-to-eat dishes.

Travelers can hire a longtail boat to explore the nearby canals, visit an orchid farm, or simply enjoy the lively atmosphere while indulging in delectable Thai street food.

III. Immersive Experiences

Boat Rides and Canal Exploration:

Exploring floating markets by boat is an essential part of the experience.

Travelers can hop aboard traditional longtail boats or paddle through the canals on kayaks for a more personal encounter with the markets.

The boat rides offer a unique perspective of the bustling activity and allow visitors to navigate the waterways, interacting with vendors and discovering hidden gems along the route.

Culinary Adventures:

Floating markets are a food lover's paradise, showcasing Thailand's diverse culinary offerings.

Travelers can indulge in mouthwatering street food, including iconic dishes like pad Thai, mango sticky rice, and tom yum soup.

Many markets offer cooking demonstrations and classes, allowing visitors to learn traditional Thai recipes and techniques from local experts.

Cultural Immersion:

Floating markets provide a glimpse into Thailand's vibrant culture and traditional way of life.

Visitors can interact with friendly locals, witness traditional handicrafts being made, and even partake in activities like fruit carving or traditional Thai massage.

Cultural performances, such as traditional music and dance shows, are often held at floating markets, offering a deeper understanding of Thai customs and traditions.

Shopping and Souvenirs:

Floating markets are a treasure trove of unique souvenirs and local products.

Travelers can browse through stalls selling handmade crafts, traditional textiles, intricate artwork, and locally sourced products like spices, herbs, and herbal remedies.

Bargaining is an integral part of the market culture, allowing visitors to engage in friendly haggling while securing memorable keepsakes.

Thailand's floating markets are not only bustling trade centers but also windows into the country's rich cultural heritage. These enchanting waterways offer an authentic experience that connects travelers with Thailand's past and present. From the iconic Damnoen Saduak Floating Market near Bangkok to the charming Amphawa Floating Market and the serene Taling Chan Floating Market, each offers its own unique atmosphere and culinary delights. Exploring these markets by boat, indulging in local delicacies, and immersing oneself in the vibrant ambiance provide an unforgettable adventure. As you plan your Thailand travel itinerary, be sure to include a visit to one of these top floating markets, where you can witness the timeless charm and traditions that continue to thrive along Thailand's waterways.

Chinatown

Thailand's diverse cultural landscape offers travelers a plethora of captivating destinations, each with its unique charm. Among these, Chinatown stands out as an exceptional and enthralling neighborhood that effortlessly combines Thai and Chinese traditions. Bursting with vibrant colors, aromatic scents, tantalizing street food, and mesmerizing temples, Chinatown in Thailand has earned its reputation as a top tourist destination. In this travel guide, we will delve into the enchanting world of Chinatown, exploring its history, cultural significance, must-see attractions, culinary delights, and practical tips to make the most of your visit.

The Historical Tapestry of Chinatown:

Thailand's Chinatown, also known as Yaowarat, traces its roots back to the early 18th century when Chinese immigrants settled in the area. Over the years, it has evolved into a bustling commercial hub and a vibrant cultural enclave. The rich historical tapestry of Chinatown is visible through its ornate architecture, traditional businesses, and the thriving Chinese community that has preserved their customs and traditions.

Cultural Fusion: Thai-Chinese Harmony:

One of the most captivating aspects of Chinatown is the harmonious blend of Thai and Chinese cultures. The influence of Chinese traditions is palpable in the neighborhood's temples, clan houses, and the practice of ancestor worship. Visitors can witness colorful festivals like Chinese New Year and the Vegetarian Festival, where the streets come alive with processions, dragon dances, and fireworks, showcasing the fusion of both cultures.

Iconic Landmarks:

Chinatown boasts an array of iconic landmarks that showcase its cultural significance and architectural splendor. The Wat Mangkon Kamalawat, a revered Chinese-Buddhist temple, is a must-visit for its intricate details, vibrant colors, and serene atmosphere. Additionally, the vibrant and bustling Talat Kao (Old Market) immerses visitors in an authentic Thai-Chinese market experience, with its vibrant stalls selling exotic fruits, spices, herbs, and traditional Chinese medicine.

Gastronomic Delights:

Chinatown is a food lover's paradise, offering an astounding variety of culinary delights. The narrow alleyways are lined with street food stalls and local eateries serving up delectable dishes that tantalize the taste buds. From the famous Thai-Chinese dish of Pad Thai to delectable dim sum, succulent roast duck, and fresh seafood, every corner of Chinatown offers a gastronomic adventure. Don't forget to savor the renowned Yaowarat Toasted Bun Ice Cream, a unique dessert that perfectly blends Chinese buns and homemade ice cream.

Shopping Extravaganza:
Chinatown's vibrant atmosphere extends to its shopping scene, offering a delightful shopping extravaganza. Sampeng Lane, the heart of Chinatown's commercial district, is a bustling market street lined with shops selling everything from textiles, clothing, accessories, and souvenirs. Bargaining skills come in handy here, as you explore the labyrinth of narrow alleys, uncovering hidden treasures and unique finds.

Hidden Gems and Off-the-Beaten-Path:
While Chinatown's main thoroughfare is undeniably captivating, exploring its hidden gems and off-the-beaten-path locations unveils

a different side of the neighborhood. Visitors can venture into the nearby Trok Itsaranuphap alley, known as the "Street of Harmony," which is home to a Hindu temple, a mosque, and a Chinese shrine, representing the diverse religious fabric of the community. Additionally, the vibrant flower market, Pak Khlong Talat, offers a sensory delight with its colorful blooms and aromatic scents.

Practical Tips for Exploring Chinatown:
To make the most of your visit to Chinatown, it is essential to keep a few practical tips in mind. Navigating the crowded streets can be overwhelming, so it is advisable to wear comfortable shoes and dress appropriately for the weather. To fully experience the culinary wonders, it's best to sample smaller portions from different food stalls. Exploring Chinatown during weekdays or on non-festive periods can offer a more relaxed experience with fewer crowds.

Chinatown in Thailand stands as a testament to the remarkable fusion of Thai and Chinese cultures. Its vibrant atmosphere, rich history, iconic landmarks, gastronomic delights, and hidden gems make it a top tourist destination for travelers seeking an authentic and captivating experience. Whether you're wandering through the bustling streets, marveling at the ornate temples, or savoring the flavors of its diverse cuisine, a visit to Thailand's Chinatown promises an unforgettable adventure, immersing you in the crossroads of two captivating cultures.

•Chiang Mai

Among the myriad of enticing destinations within the country, Chiang Mai reigns supreme as a top tourist hotspot. Nestled in the picturesque mountains of northern Thailand, Chiang Mai boasts a unique blend of ancient temples, lush landscapes, traditional markets, and a thriving arts scene. This travel guide aims to provide an in-depth exploration of Chiang Mai, shedding light on its rich heritage, must-visit attractions, delightful cuisine, and diverse activities, helping you plan an unforgettable adventure in this enchanting city.

Discovering Chiang Mai's Rich Heritage

1.1 Historical Significance

Chiang Mai holds a significant place in Thai history, having been the capital of the Lanna Kingdom from the 13th to the 18th century. This rich heritage is still evident today through the city's magnificent temples, ancient walls, and moats. Exploring the historic center allows visitors to immerse themselves in the city's past and appreciate its cultural legacy.

1.2 Temples and Sacred Sites

Chiang Mai is home to over 300 temples, each bearing its unique architectural style and historical importance. Wat Phra That Doi Suthep, perched on a mountainside, offers breathtaking panoramic views of the city and is considered the most sacred temple in the region. Other notable temples include Wat Chedi Luang, known for its towering pagoda, and Wat Phra Singh, housing the revered Phra Buddha Sihing image.

Must-Visit Attractions in Chiang Mai

2.1 The Old City

Enclosed by ancient walls and a moat, Chiang Mai's Old City is a treasure trove of cultural and historical landmarks. Strolling through its narrow streets, visitors can admire traditional teak houses, discover hidden temples, and indulge in local street food. The Sunday Walking Street Market, stretching along Ratchadamnoen Road, is a must-visit, offering a vibrant tapestry of arts, crafts, and local delicacies.

2.2 Doi Suthep-Pui National Park

Escape the city's bustle and immerse yourself in the natural splendor of Doi Suthep-Pui National Park. Located just a short drive from the city, this mountainous sanctuary is renowned for its lush forests, cascading waterfalls, and diverse wildlife. The park also houses the revered Wat Phra That Doi Suthep, making it an ideal destination for nature enthusiasts and spiritual seekers alike.

2.3 Elephant Sanctuaries

For a truly unforgettable experience, visit one of Chiang Mai's ethical elephant sanctuaries. These sanctuaries provide a humane alternative to elephant riding, allowing visitors to observe and interact with these gentle giants in a responsible and sustainable manner. Spend a day feeding, bathing, and learning about the conservation efforts dedicated to protecting these magnificent creatures.

Cultural Immersion and Experiences

3.1 Thai Cooking Classes

Embark on a gastronomic adventure by enrolling in a traditional Thai cooking class. Chiang Mai offers an array of culinary schools where you can learn to prepare mouthwatering dishes like Pad Thai, green curry, and mango sticky rice. Delve into the vibrant world of Thai spices and flavors, and bring home the secrets of authentic Thai cuisine.

3.2 Yi Peng Lantern Festival

Timing your visit to coincide with the Yi Peng Lantern Festival is an opportunity to witness a spectacle like no other. Celebrated annually, this event sees thousands of paper lanterns released into the night sky, illuminating the city with their soft glow. The festival also involves traditional performances, music, and a sense of communal spirit that is deeply ingrained in Thai culture.

Culinary Delights of Chiang Mai

4.1 Khao Soi

No visit to Chiang Mai is complete without savoring a bowl of Khao Soi. This iconic dish combines egg noodles in a rich coconut curry broth, topped with crispy fried noodles, shallots, and lime. The contrasting textures and flavors make Khao Soi a true culinary delight and a must-try dish for food enthusiasts.

4.2 Street Food Exploration

Chiang Mai's bustling street markets offer a myriad of tantalizing street food options. From savory skewers of grilled meat to delectable mango sticky rice, the street food scene in Chiang Mai is a paradise for food lovers. Sample local favorites like sai ua (northern Thai sausage) and khao kha moo (stewed pork leg) while immersing yourself in the lively atmosphere of the night markets.

Outdoor Adventures and Nature

5.1 Trekking and Hill Tribe Visits

The verdant landscapes surrounding Chiang Mai are perfect for outdoor enthusiasts seeking adventure. Join a guided trek through the lush jungles, trekking to remote hill tribe villages and immersing yourself in their fascinating cultures. Engage with the locals, witness their traditional way of life, and discover the natural beauty that abounds in this region.

5.2 Doi Inthanon National Park

As Thailand's highest peak, Doi Inthanon offers a cool retreat from the city's tropical climate. Explore the park's hiking trails, visit picturesque waterfalls, and marvel at the stunning flora and fauna that thrive in this mountainous sanctuary. Don't miss the opportunity to witness the breathtaking sunrise from the summit and explore the Royal Chedis, dedicated to the King and Queen of Thailand.

Chiang Mai, with its rich heritage, cultural abundance, and natural beauty, is a top tourist destination in Thailand. From its ancient temples and historic landmarks to its vibrant markets, delicious cuisine, and outdoor adventures, the city offers a diverse range of experiences that cater to every traveler's preferences. Whether you seek cultural immersion, culinary delights, or nature exploration, Chiang Mai is sure to leave an indelible mark on your heart and soul. Plan your journey to this captivating city and embark on a memorable adventure through the enchanting landscapes and warm hospitality of Chiang Mai, the cultural haven of northern Thailand.

Wat Phra That Doi Suthep

Thailand, often referred to as the "Land of Smiles," is a country known for its rich cultural heritage and stunning natural beauty. Among the countless attractions that captivate visitors, Wat Phra That Doi Suthep stands as a shining gem in the northern region of the country. As one of Thailand's most revered and iconic Buddhist temples, Wat Phra That Doi Suthep has attracted travelers from all corners of the globe. This comprehensive Thailand travel guide will delve into the captivating history, cultural significance, breathtaking beauty, and practical information of this magnificent temple, providing you with all you need to know for an unforgettable visit.

I. Historical Significance:

Nestled on the slopes of Doi Suthep mountain, approximately 15 kilometers from Chiang Mai, Wat Phra That Doi Suthep boasts a rich history that dates back over 700 years. According to legend, a relic of the Buddha, believed to be his shoulder bone, was mounted on a sacred white elephant that ascended the mountain before trumpeting three times and eventually passing away. This miraculous event was interpreted as a divine sign, leading to the establishment of the temple in 1383. The intricate details of its construction and the spiritual devotion embedded in its foundations have made Wat Phra That Doi Suthep a sanctuary of immense importance for Thai Buddhists.

II. Architectural Grandeur:

The architectural brilliance of Wat Phra That Doi Suthep leaves visitors awestruck. Ascending the Naga staircase, adorned with intricate serpent-like sculptures, visitors are greeted by the stunning golden chedi, or stupa, which stands as the centerpiece of the temple.

The chedi is lavishly embellished with gold leaf and encrusted with precious gems, while its uppermost tier showcases the revered relic of the Buddha. The outer area of the temple complex is adorned with various pagodas, shrines, and intricate murals, each reflecting the rich cultural heritage of the Lanna Kingdom. The blend of traditional Lanna and Sri Lankan architectural styles creates a captivating ambiance that immerses visitors in a spiritual and historical journey.

III. Cultural Significance and Religious Practices:

Wat Phra That Doi Suthep remains an active Buddhist temple, serving as a spiritual center for both monks and devotees. Visitors have the opportunity to witness the local Buddhist community engaging in prayer, meditation, and other religious rituals. The serene environment, the sound of ringing bells, and the scent of incense create a tranquil atmosphere that fosters introspection and spiritual contemplation. Observing the devotees' dedication and participating in the religious practices offer a unique insight into Thai Buddhism, making Wat Phra That Doi Suthep an invaluable cultural experience.

IV. Panoramic Views and Natural Beauty:

Apart from its cultural and religious significance, Wat Phra That Doi Suthep offers breathtaking panoramic views of Chiang Mai and its surrounding landscapes. As visitors reach the temple's terrace, they are rewarded with a captivating vista of the city, lush green mountains, and the distant Ping River. The refreshing mountain air and the harmonious blend of natural and man-made beauty provide a welcome respite from the bustling city below. Exploring the temple grounds further reveals meticulously maintained gardens, serene water features, and the tranquil sounds of nature, inviting visitors to embrace the tranquility of this sacred space.

V. Practical Information:

Getting There: Wat Phra That Doi Suthep can be reached by hiring a songthaew (shared red truck taxi), taking a private taxi, or joining a guided tour from Chiang Mai. The journey typically takes around 30-45 minutes.

Dress Code: As a place of worship, modest attire is required. Visitors should ensure their shoulders and knees are covered. Sarongs and scarves are available for rent at the entrance for those who need them.

Operating Hours: The temple is open daily from early morning until late evening, allowing visitors to enjoy the temple's beauty at different times of the day. However, note that some areas may be restricted during specific religious ceremonies or events.

Best Time to Visit: To avoid crowds and enjoy a peaceful atmosphere, it's recommended to visit Wat Phra That Doi Suthep early in the morning or during weekdays. Additionally, visiting during Buddhist holidays or important festivals, such as Songkran (Thai New Year) or Loy Krathong, can provide a unique cultural experience.

Services and Facilities: The temple complex provides facilities such as restrooms, drinking water stations, and a small market where visitors can purchase souvenirs, religious artifacts, and traditional handicrafts.

Wat Phra That Doi Suthep represents the essence of Thailand's spiritual and cultural heritage, offering visitors a glimpse into the country's deep-rooted traditions. Its historical significance, architectural grandeur, cultural practices, breathtaking views, and tranquil surroundings combine to create an unforgettable experience. A visit to this iconic temple is an essential part of any Thailand travel itinerary, allowing travelers to immerse themselves in the beauty, spirituality, and profound cultural richness that the Land of Smiles has to offer.

Old City Temples

Thailand, known as the Land of Smiles, is a captivating country with a rich cultural heritage. Among its many attractions, the Old City Temples stand out as a must-visit destination for travelers seeking an immersive experience into Thailand's spiritual and historical roots. This comprehensive travel guide delves into the allure of the Old City Temples, exploring their significance, architectural marvels, and the unique cultural practices associated with these sacred sites. Join us on this enchanting journey through Thailand's ancient treasures.

Discovering the Old City:

Located in the heart of Bangkok, the Old City is a historic area that served as the capital of the Kingdom of Siam for over four centuries. This vibrant district is home to a cluster of magnificent temples, each bearing witness to Thailand's glorious past. As you wander through the narrow streets and bustling markets, you will be transported to a bygone era, immersed in the sights, sounds, and scents of Thailand's cultural tapestry.

Wat Phra Kaew - The Temple of the Emerald Buddha:

Among the most revered temples in Thailand, Wat Phra Kaew holds a special place in the hearts of the Thai people. Housed within the grounds of the Grand Palace, this temple is home to the magnificent Emerald Buddha, a revered icon believed to bring prosperity and good fortune. The temple's intricate architecture, adorned with exquisite murals and gilded sculptures, mesmerizes visitors with its grandeur and spiritual aura.

Wat Pho - The Temple of the Reclining Buddha:

Adjacent to the Grand Palace, Wat Pho is a temple renowned for its awe-inspiring

Reclining Buddha statue. Measuring an astonishing 46 meters in length, this gold-plated marvel captivates all who lay eyes upon it. Besides this remarkable centerpiece, Wat Pho is also a hub for traditional Thai massage, offering weary travelers a chance to relax and rejuvenate amidst the tranquil temple grounds.

Wat Arun - The Temple of Dawn:
Standing gracefully on the banks of the Chao Phraya River, Wat Arun is a breathtaking temple that showcases a blend of Khmer and Thai architectural styles. Its towering spires, adorned with intricate porcelain tiles, glisten in the sunlight, creating a dazzling spectacle. Ascend the temple's central prang for a panoramic view of Bangkok's skyline, especially mesmerizing during sunset.

Wat Saket - The Golden Mount:
Situated atop an artificial hill, Wat Saket, also known as the Golden Mount, offers a serene escape from the bustling city below. As you ascend the winding staircase, surrounded by lush greenery and ancient bells, you'll be rewarded with panoramic vistas of Bangkok. The temple's golden chedi, housing sacred

relics, symbolizes the spiritual journey to enlightenment.

Wat Benchamabophit - The Marble Temple:

Known as the Marble Temple, Wat Benchamabophit is a stunning testament to Thai craftsmanship. Constructed from imported Italian marble, this temple is a visual feast, with intricate detailing and elegant design. The serene atmosphere and meticulously maintained gardens make it an ideal place for meditation and contemplation.

Wat Rong Khun - The White Temple:

Located in Chiang Rai, Wat Rong Khun stands out from the traditional Thai temples with its surreal and unconventional design. The temple's exterior, entirely clad in white, symbolizes purity and enlightenment. Intricate, contemporary murals inside the temple depict pop culture references and spiritual teachings, creating a unique fusion of ancient and modern art.

Cultural Significance and Practices:

Visiting the Old City Temples goes beyond admiring their architectural splendor; it provides an opportunity to witness and engage with Thailand's vibrant cultural practices. Observe locals making merit, offering prayers, and participating in traditional rituals. Witness the vibrant festivals celebrated at these temples, such as Songkran (Thai New Year) and Loy Krathong (Festival of Lights), to immerse yourself fully in Thai traditions.

Practical Information:
To make the most of your visit to the Old City Temples, consider the following practical tips. Respect local customs and dress modestly, covering your shoulders and knees. As these temples are sacred sites, maintain a quiet and respectful demeanor. Engage the services of a knowledgeable local guide who can provide historical insights and cultural context.

Exploring the Old City Temples in Thailand is a transformative experience that allows travelers to connect with the country's spiritual and historical roots. From the grandeur of Wat Phra Kaew to the serenity of Wat Saket, each temple offers a unique glimpse into Thailand's rich cultural tapestry. By immersing yourself in the rituals and traditions associated with these sacred sites, you'll gain a deeper appreciation for Thailand's spiritual heritage. Embark on this enchanting journey and create lifelong memories as you explore the top tourist destination of Thailand's Old City Temples.

Elephant Nature Park

Thailand, renowned for its vibrant culture, stunning beaches, and mouthwatering cuisine, has emerged as a top tourist destination. Amidst the countless attractions that beckon travelers, one place stands out as a must-visit destination: Elephant Nature Park. Nestled in the picturesque mountains of Northern Thailand, this sanctuary has gained international acclaim for its commitment to wildlife conservation and ethical elephant tourism. In this Thailand travel guide, we delve into the allure of Elephant Nature Park, highlighting its rich history, engaging activities, and the unparalleled experience it offers visitors.

History and Mission :

Elephant Nature Park was founded in the 1990s by Lek Chailert, a passionate advocate for elephant welfare. Lek witnessed the mistreatment and abuse suffered by elephants throughout Thailand's tourism industry, leading her to establish the park as a safe haven for these gentle giants. With a mission to rescue, rehabilitate, and provide a natural environment for elephants, the park aims to educate visitors about the importance of conservation and responsible tourism.

Ethical Elephant Tourism :

One of the key factors that sets Elephant Nature Park apart from traditional elephant camps is its commitment to ethical tourism practices. Unlike establishments that exploit elephants for entertainment, this sanctuary prioritizes the well-being and happiness of the animals. Visitors have the opportunity to observe these majestic creatures in their natural habitat without any invasive interactions. Elephant rides, shows, and other unnatural activities are strictly prohibited.

Engaging Activities :

A visit to Elephant Nature Park offers an array of engaging activities that provide an up-close and personal encounter with the elephants.

Visitors can observe and participate in their daily routines, including feeding them, walking alongside them, and even bathing them in the river. These activities are designed to create a positive and stress-free environment for both elephants and visitors, fostering a deeper connection and understanding of these incredible creatures.

Wildlife Conservation Efforts :

Elephant Nature Park is not just a sanctuary for elephants; it is also actively involved in broader wildlife conservation efforts. The park provides a home for other rescued animals, such as dogs, cats, and water buffaloes, promoting coexistence and environmental harmony. Additionally, Elephant Nature Park contributes to community development by supporting local initiatives and offering employment opportunities to nearby villages, thereby benefiting the region as a whole.

Educational Experiences :

Beyond its conservation efforts, Elephant Nature Park serves as an educational hub for visitors. The park's knowledgeable staff, often referred to as "elephant whisperers," offer valuable insights into elephant behavior, their natural habitats, and the challenges they face in the wild. Informative presentations and interactive sessions allow visitors to gain a deeper appreciation for these magnificent animals and the importance of their preservation.

Visitor Impact and Volunteering Opportunities :

A visit to Elephant Nature Park is not just a passive experience; it is an opportunity for visitors to actively contribute to the park's mission. The park offers various volunteering programs where individuals can work alongside the staff, assisting with tasks such as feeding, bathing, and cleaning the elephant enclosures. These programs provide a unique chance to make a positive impact while forming lifelong memories.

Elephant Nature Park stands as a shining example of ethical tourism and wildlife conservation in Thailand. Its dedication to providing a safe haven for elephants, coupled with engaging activities and educational experiences, make it a top tourist destination for those seeking an authentic and responsible wildlife encounter. By supporting Elephant Nature Park, visitors not only contribute to the well-being of elephants and other animals but also actively participate in promoting sustainable and ethical tourism practices. A visit to this remarkable sanctuary is not just an unforgettable experience; it is an opportunity to make a difference and foster a brighter future for Thailand's wildlife.

Sunday Night Walking Street Market

Thailand, often referred to as the "Land of Smiles," is a captivating country that boasts a rich cultural heritage, stunning natural landscapes, and vibrant local markets. Among these markets, the Sunday Night Walking Street Market stands out as a must-visit destination for tourists. Located in the historical center of a prominent city, this bustling market offers a sensory feast of local delicacies, unique handicrafts, live performances, and an unforgettable cultural experience. In this Thailand travel guide, we will delve into the enchanting world of the Sunday Night Walking Street Market, highlighting its historical significance, key attractions, culinary delights, shopping opportunities, and tips for making the most of your visit.

I. Historical Significance and Location :

The Sunday Night Walking Street Market, also known as the Walking Street Market or simply the Walking Street, is situated in the heart of Chiang Mai, a captivating city in Northern Thailand. Chiang Mai, renowned for its ancient temples and traditional Lanna architecture, provides the perfect backdrop for this vibrant market. The market takes place along Ratchadamnoen Road, which stretches from Tha Phae Gate to Wat Phra Singh, two iconic landmarks in the city.

The roots of the Sunday Night Walking Street Market can be traced back to the old trade routes that connected Chiang Mai to neighboring countries such as Myanmar, Laos, and China. These routes brought a diverse range of cultures and influences, which contributed to the unique blend of arts, crafts, and culinary traditions found in the market today. The market has evolved over the years to become a hub for local artisans, performers, and food vendors, attracting both locals and tourists alike.

II. Key Attractions :

Cultural Performances: Immerse yourself in the vibrant Thai culture by enjoying the captivating performances that take place throughout the market. From traditional music and dance shows to puppetry and martial arts demonstrations, the Sunday Night Walking Street Market offers a diverse array of entertainment options.

Handicrafts and Artwork: The market is a treasure trove for art enthusiasts and collectors. Local artisans showcase their skills through a wide range of handmade products, including intricately carved wooden sculptures, handwoven textiles, ceramic pottery, and exquisite jewelry. Exploring the stalls provides a unique opportunity to witness the craftsmanship and creativity of the Thai people.

Temples and Spiritual Sites: Chiang Mai is home to numerous ancient temples, and the Sunday Night Walking Street Market is no exception. Along the market route, visitors can explore architectural gems such as Wat Phra Singh, a revered Buddhist temple known for its stunning golden pagoda, and Wat Chedi Luang, which houses the remnants of a massive pagoda that dates back to the 15th century.

Street Food Delights: A visit to the Sunday Night Walking Street Market would be incomplete without indulging in the tantalizing street food offerings. From aromatic curries and grilled skewers to freshly made noodles and exotic fruits, the market boasts a vast array of culinary delights. Adventurous eaters can sample local favorites like khao soi (curried noodles), sai oua (northern Thai sausage), and mango sticky rice, while those with milder taste buds can savor mouthwatering grilled meats and delectable desserts.

III. Shopping Opportunities :

The Sunday Night Walking Street Market is a shopaholic's paradise, offering a wide variety of goods that cater to all tastes and budgets. Here are some of the shopping highlights:

Handicrafts and Souvenirs: The market is a haven for those seeking authentic Thai handicrafts and souvenirs. Visitors can find beautifully crafted items such as silk scarves, hand-painted umbrellas, lacquerware, silverware, and traditional hill tribe textiles. These unique and culturally rich products make for memorable keepsakes or gifts for loved ones back home.

Fashion and Accessories: Fashion enthusiasts will appreciate the diverse range of clothing and accessories available at the market. From trendy clothing inspired by Thai fashion designers to traditional hill tribe garments, there is something for everyone. Additionally, shoppers can browse through a selection of accessories like handmade jewelry, bags, and footwear to complete their look.

Home Decor and Antiques: The market is an ideal place to discover one-of-a-kind home decor items and antiques. From antique furniture and intricately designed lamps to vintage ceramics and decorative pieces, the market offers a glimpse into the rich artistic heritage of the region. These unique items can add a touch of Thai elegance to any home.

Local Produce and Natural Products: For those interested in natural and locally sourced products, the Sunday Night Walking Street Market has an array of offerings. Visitors can find organic skincare products, herbal remedies, essential oils, and traditional Thai massage balms. Fresh fruits, spices, and teas are also available for those looking to take a taste of Thailand home with them.

IV. *Tips for Making the Most of Your Visit :*

To ensure a memorable experience at the Sunday Night Walking Street Market, consider the following tips:

Arrive Early: The market tends to get crowded as the night progresses, so arriving early allows you to explore the stalls more comfortably and leisurely. It also provides an opportunity to witness the transformation of the street as vendors set up their displays.

Bargaining: Bargaining is a common practice in Thai markets, including the Sunday Night Walking Street Market. While it may not be appropriate or expected at all stalls, feel free to negotiate prices with individual vendors, especially for non-fixed-price items such as handicrafts or clothing. Remember to approach bargaining with a friendly and respectful attitude.

Explore Side Streets: While the main stretch of Ratchadamnoen Road is the heart of the market, don't forget to venture into the side streets and alleyways. These hidden gems often offer unique finds and a more intimate shopping experience.

Stay Hydrated and Try Local Treats: The market can be quite crowded and walking-intensive, so it's important to stay hydrated. Numerous vendors sell refreshing beverages, including freshly squeezed fruit juices and iced teas. Additionally, be adventurous and try some local treats and snacks along the way.

Respect Local Customs: Thailand is a country with rich cultural traditions, and it's important to respect local customs and etiquette. Dress modestly, remove your shoes when entering temples or certain shops, and be mindful of appropriate behavior when observing religious ceremonies or cultural performances.

The Sunday Night Walking Street Market in Chiang Mai, Thailand, is a vibrant and enchanting destination that offers an immersive experience into the country's rich cultural heritage. With its diverse range of attractions, including cultural performances, handicrafts, culinary delights, and shopping opportunities, the market truly embodies the essence of Thai culture. Exploring the market's historical significance, witnessing traditional arts and crafts, savoring delicious street food, and discovering unique souvenirs are just a few of the many experiences that await visitors. The Sunday Night Walking Street Market undoubtedly deserves its place as a top tourist destination in Thailand, providing an unforgettable journey into the heart and soul of this fascinating country.

•Phuket

Nestled in the turquoise waters of the Andaman Sea, Phuket stands as a premier tourist destination in Thailand. Renowned for its idyllic beaches, vibrant nightlife, and rich cultural heritage, this tropical island offers a myriad of experiences to travelers from across the globe. With its pristine shores, lush landscapes, and warm hospitality, Phuket has rightfully earned its place as one of Thailand's top tourist destinations. In this comprehensive Thailand travel guide, we will delve into the enchanting allure of Phuket, exploring its natural wonders, cultural treasures, and unforgettable experiences.

Beaches and Island Getaways:

Phuket boasts an extensive coastline adorned with postcard-perfect beaches that cater to all preferences. Patong Beach, the most famous and lively beach, is the hub of entertainment and nightlife. Karon and Kata beaches offer a more relaxed atmosphere, perfect for families and couples. For those seeking tranquility, the unspoiled beauty of Nai Harn Beach and Surin Beach beckon. Additionally, the nearby Phi Phi Islands, Similan Islands, and Phang Nga Bay offer breathtaking scenery, crystal-clear waters, and exceptional snorkeling and diving opportunities.

Cultural Treasures:

Beyond its stunning natural beauty, Phuket also boasts a rich cultural heritage. The Old Town of Phuket City provides a glimpse into the island's past, with its Sino-Portuguese architecture, colorful buildings, and bustling markets. Wat Chalong, the island's largest and most revered Buddhist temple, showcases intricate Thai architecture and offers a serene atmosphere for spiritual exploration. The Phuket Thaihua Museum provides fascinating insights into the island's history and the influence of Chinese immigrants.

Water Sports and Outdoor Adventures:

Phuket offers an abundance of thrilling activities for adventure enthusiasts. From jet skiing and parasailing to windsurfing and paddleboarding, the island's azure waters provide endless opportunities for aquatic fun. For those seeking adrenaline-pumping experiences, jungle trekking, ATV rides, and ziplining adventures in the lush hinterlands of Phuket are available. Elephant sanctuaries allow visitors to interact with these majestic creatures in an ethical and responsible manner.

Vibrant Nightlife and Entertainment:

Phuket's vibrant nightlife is legendary. Patong Beach comes alive after dark, offering an array of nightclubs, bars, and live music venues. The infamous Bangla Road is the epicenter of Phuket's nightlife, with its neon lights, street performances, and pulsating atmosphere. For a more laid-back experience, the beach clubs of Kamala and Surin are perfect for enjoying a sunset cocktail while taking in the panoramic views.

Wellness and Relaxation:

Phuket has emerged as a premier wellness destination, offering world-class spas, yoga retreats, and detox centers. The island's serene ambiance, coupled with the healing properties of traditional Thai massages and holistic therapies, make it an ideal place to rejuvenate the mind, body, and soul. Many resorts and retreat centers provide tailored wellness programs, allowing visitors to indulge in meditation, yoga, and organic cuisine.

Gastronomic Delights:

The culinary scene in Phuket is a delightful fusion of Thai flavors, international cuisine, and fresh seafood. From vibrant street food markets to high-end restaurants, the island caters to all taste buds. The night markets of Phuket Town and Patong offer an opportunity to savor local delicacies like pad Thai, green curry, and mango sticky rice. Additionally, the floating seafood restaurants of Rawai Beach serve up mouthwatering seafood dishes, including the iconic Phuket-style lobster.

Shopping and Souvenirs:

Phuket is a shopper's paradise, with a wide range of options to explore. The bustling markets of Phuket Town and Patong offer a treasure trove of souvenirs, handicrafts, clothing, and accessories. For luxury shopping, the Jungceylon Mall in Patong features international brands, while the Central Festival

Phuket in Phuket Town caters to both high-end and affordable fashion. Traditional Thai silk, intricate wood carvings, and locally produced ceramics are popular souvenirs to take home.

Phuket, with its stunning natural beauty, vibrant culture, and diverse experiences, captivates the hearts of travelers seeking a tropical paradise. Whether lounging on pristine beaches, immersing oneself in cultural heritage, embarking on exhilarating adventures, or indulging in exquisite cuisine, Phuket offers an unforgettable journey for every visitor. With its warm hospitality and unmatched charm, it is no wonder that Phuket remains one of Thailand's top tourist destinations, welcoming millions of travelers year after year. Embark on your own Phuket adventure and discover the magic of this paradise island.

Patong Beach

Thailand, renowned for its mesmerizing landscapes, vibrant culture, and warm hospitality, is a dream destination for travelers worldwide. Among its myriad attractions, Patong Beach shines brightly as one of the top tourist hotspots in this enchanting country. Situated on the picturesque island of Phuket, Patong Beach is an idyllic tropical paradise that offers an unforgettable holiday experience. With its stunning sandy shores, azure waters, pulsating nightlife, and a wealth of recreational activities, Patong Beach has firmly established itself as a must-visit destination in Thailand. In this comprehensive travel guide, we will delve into the captivating allure of Patong Beach, exploring its natural beauty, cultural highlights, thrilling adventures, and the myriad of opportunities it offers to create cherished memories.

Geographical Location and Accessibility :

Patong Beach is located on the western coast of the island of Phuket, in the Andaman Sea. Its strategic location, approximately 15 kilometers from Phuket Town and 40 kilometers from Phuket International Airport, makes it easily accessible to travelers from all corners of the globe. Upon arrival at the airport, visitors can conveniently reach Patong Beach via taxis, private transfers, or shared minivans. Additionally, there are numerous tour operators that provide shuttle services, ensuring a hassle-free journey to this tropical paradise.

Natural Beauty and Beachfront Splendor :

Patong Beach entices visitors with its breathtaking natural beauty, combining pristine sandy shores, crystal-clear turquoise waters, and a backdrop of lush green hills. Stretching for nearly 3.5 kilometers, the beach offers ample space for sun-seekers to unwind, soak up the tropical sunshine, and revel in the refreshing ocean breeze. The gentle waves and shallow waters make it an ideal spot for swimming and a variety of water sports activities.

As the sun begins to set, the beach transforms into a magical setting. The vibrant hues of the sky blend seamlessly with the calm ocean, creating a captivating vista for romantic strolls along the shore. Patong Beach also offers a mesmerizing viewpoint from which visitors can witness the spectacular sunsets that paint the horizon in a kaleidoscope of colors.

Vibrant Nightlife and Entertainment :

Apart from its natural splendor, Patong Beach is renowned for its vibrant nightlife, making it an exhilarating playground for party enthusiasts. The infamous Bangla Road, situated just a stone's throw away from the beach, is a bustling hub of entertainment, teeming with clubs, bars, and discos that pulsate with music and energy until the early hours of the morning. Visitors can indulge in a night of revelry, dance to the beats of international DJs, and experience the electrifying atmosphere that has earned Patong Beach its reputation as the party capital of Phuket.

For those seeking a more relaxed ambiance, the beachfront bars and lounges offer a tranquil setting to unwind with a refreshing cocktail in hand. Enjoying a drink while gazing out at the expansive ocean vista is a perfect way to end a day of exploration on the beach.

Cultural Highlights and Local Attractions :

Patong Beach is not only a haven for beach lovers but also a gateway to explore the rich cultural heritage of Thailand. Visitors can immerse themselves in the vibrant local culture by exploring the temples and shrines that dot the landscape. The nearby Wat Patong and Wat Suwan Khiri Khet are two noteworthy examples, exuding a serene ambiance and showcasing exquisite architectural designs.

For an authentic Thai experience, travelers can visit the lively Patong Market, where a plethora of stalls offer an array of local delicacies, handicrafts, and souvenirs. Exploring the market provides a unique opportunity to interact with friendly locals, sample mouthwatering street food, and purchase traditional Thai products.

Adventure and Recreational Activities :
Thrill-seekers and adventure enthusiasts will find an abundance of exhilarating activities to partake in at Patong Beach. From parasailing and jet-skiing to scuba diving and snorkeling, the azure waters offer an underwater playground waiting to be explored. Professional diving schools and tour operators cater to both beginners and experienced divers, providing opportunities to discover vibrant coral reefs and encounter a myriad of marine life.

For those seeking a bird's-eye view of the stunning coastline, parasailing provides an adrenaline-pumping experience. Suspended high above the beach, visitors can savor panoramic vistas of Patong's tropical beauty.

Beyond the beach, visitors can embark on a thrilling zip-lining adventure through the lush rainforests surrounding Patong. Flying through the treetops on a network of zip lines and suspended bridges offers an exhilarating perspective of Phuket's dense vegetation and cascading waterfalls.

Accommodation and Gastronomy :

Patong Beach offers an extensive range of accommodation options to suit all budgets and preferences. From luxury resorts and boutique hotels to budget-friendly guesthouses, visitors can find a comfortable stay that caters to their needs. Many establishments provide direct beach access, ensuring a seamless transition from relaxation to exploration.

The dining scene in Patong Beach is equally diverse, with a multitude of restaurants, cafes, and street food stalls serving delectable Thai cuisine as well as international delicacies. From freshly caught seafood to aromatic curries, visitors can embark on a culinary journey that tantalizes the taste buds and immerses them in the flavors of Thailand.

Patong Beach, with its captivating beauty, vibrant nightlife, and an array of activities, is undeniably a top tourist destination in

Thailand. Whether seeking relaxation, adventure, cultural immersion, or lively entertainment, this tropical paradise caters to every traveler's desires. From the stunning natural landscapes to the pulsating energy of Bangla Road, Patong Beach captivates visitors with its unique charm and promises an unforgettable holiday experience. So, pack your bags, immerse yourself in the enchantment of Patong Beach, and create memories that will last a lifetime in this mesmerizing corner of Thailand's tropical paradise.

Phi Phi Islands

Thailand, renowned for its mesmerizing landscapes, vibrant culture, and warm hospitality, is a dream destination for travelers worldwide. Among its myriad attractions, Patong Beach shines brightly as one of the top tourist hotspots in this enchanting country. Situated on the picturesque island of Phuket, Patong Beach is an idyllic tropical paradise that offers an unforgettable holiday experience. With its stunning sandy shores, azure waters, pulsating nightlife, and a wealth of recreational activities, Patong Beach has firmly established itself as a must-visit destination in Thailand. In this comprehensive travel guide, we will delve into the captivating allure of Patong Beach, exploring its natural beauty, cultural highlights, thrilling adventures, and the myriad of opportunities it offers to create cherished memories.

Geographical Location and Accessibility :

Patong Beach is located on the western coast of the island of Phuket, in the Andaman Sea. Its strategic location, approximately 15 kilometers from Phuket Town and 40 kilometers from Phuket International Airport, makes it easily accessible to travelers from all corners of the globe. Upon arrival at the airport, visitors can conveniently reach Patong Beach via taxis, private transfers, or shared minivans. Additionally, there are numerous tour operators that provide shuttle services, ensuring a hassle-free journey to this tropical paradise.

Natural Beauty and Beachfront Splendor :

Patong Beach entices visitors with its breathtaking natural beauty, combining pristine sandy shores, crystal-clear turquoise waters, and a backdrop of lush green hills. Stretching for nearly 3.5 kilometers, the beach offers ample space for sun-seekers to unwind, soak up the tropical sunshine, and revel in the refreshing ocean breeze. The gentle waves and shallow waters make it an ideal spot for swimming and a variety of water sports activities.

As the sun begins to set, the beach transforms into a magical setting. The vibrant hues of the sky blend seamlessly with the calm ocean, creating a captivating vista for romantic strolls along the shore. Patong Beach also offers a mesmerizing viewpoint from which visitors can witness the spectacular sunsets that paint the horizon in a kaleidoscope of colors.

Vibrant Nightlife and Entertainment :
Apart from its natural splendor, Patong Beach is renowned for its vibrant nightlife, making it an exhilarating playground for party enthusiasts. The infamous Bangla Road, situated just a stone's throw away from the beach, is a bustling hub of entertainment, teeming with clubs, bars, and discos that pulsate with music and energy until the early hours of the morning. Visitors can indulge in a

night of revelry, dance to the beats of international DJs, and experience the electrifying atmosphere that has earned Patong Beach its reputation as the party capital of Phuket.

For those seeking a more relaxed ambiance, the beachfront bars and lounges offer a tranquil setting to unwind with a refreshing cocktail in hand. Enjoying a drink while gazing out at the expansive ocean vista is a perfect way to end a day of exploration on the beach.

Cultural Highlights and Local Attractions :

Patong Beach is not only a haven for beach lovers but also a gateway to explore the rich cultural heritage of Thailand. Visitors can immerse themselves in the vibrant local culture by exploring the temples and shrines that dot the landscape. The nearby Wat Patong and Wat Suwan Khiri Khet are two noteworthy examples, exuding a serene ambiance and showcasing exquisite architectural designs.

For an authentic Thai experience, travelers can visit the lively Patong Market, where a plethora of stalls offer an array of local delicacies, handicrafts, and souvenirs. Exploring the market provides a unique opportunity to interact with friendly locals, sample mouthwatering street food, and purchase traditional Thai products.

Adventure and Recreational Activities :
Thrill-seekers and adventure enthusiasts will find an abundance of exhilarating activities to partake in at Patong Beach. From parasailing and jet-skiing to scuba diving and snorkeling, the azure waters offer an underwater playground waiting to be explored. Professional diving schools and tour operators cater to both beginners and experienced divers, providing opportunities to discover vibrant coral reefs and encounter a myriad of marine life.

For those seeking a bird's-eye view of the stunning coastline, parasailing provides an adrenaline-pumping experience. Suspended high above the beach, visitors can savor panoramic vistas of Patong's tropical beauty.

Beyond the beach, visitors can embark on a thrilling zip-lining adventure through the lush rainforests surrounding Patong. Flying through the treetops on a network of zip lines and suspended bridges offers an exhilarating perspective of Phuket's dense vegetation and cascading waterfalls.

Accommodation and Gastronomy :
Patong Beach offers an extensive range of accommodation options to suit all budgets and preferences. From luxury resorts and boutique hotels to budget-friendly guesthouses, visitors can find a comfortable stay that caters to their needs. Many establishments provide direct beach access, ensuring a seamless transition from relaxation to exploration.

The dining scene in Patong Beach is equally diverse, with a multitude of restaurants, cafes, and street food stalls serving delectable Thai cuisine as well as international delicacies. From freshly caught seafood to aromatic curries, visitors can embark on a culinary journey that tantalizes the taste buds and immerses them in the flavors of Thailand.

Patong Beach, with its captivating beauty, vibrant nightlife, and an array of activities, is undeniably a top tourist destination in Thailand. Whether seeking relaxation, adventure, cultural immersion, or lively entertainment, this tropical paradise caters to every traveler's desires. From the stunning natural landscapes to the pulsating energy of Bangla Road, Patong Beach captivates visitors with its unique charm and promises an unforgettable holiday experience. So, pack your bags, immerse yourself in the enchantment of Patong Beach, and create memories that will last a lifetime in this mesmerizing corner of Thailand's tropical paradise.

Big Buddha

Thailand, known for its vibrant culture, rich history, and stunning landscapes, offers an abundance of attractions to explore. Among its numerous landmarks, the Big Buddha stands out as an iconic and sacred monument that captivates the hearts of locals and tourists alike. Located in various parts of the country, the Big Buddha statues represent the reverence and spiritual devotion deeply rooted in Thai culture. This comprehensive travel guide will focus on the Big Buddha in Thailand, shedding light on its significance, historical background, architectural marvel, and the enriching experiences it offers to visitors.

Historical Background and Cultural Significance:

The Big Buddha, also known as Phra Buddha Maha Nawamin, holds great cultural and religious importance in Thailand. Buddhism plays a fundamental role in Thai society, and the Big Buddha represents the embodiment of its teachings. These colossal statues are revered symbols of peace, serenity, and enlightenment, reflecting the core principles of Buddhism.

The construction of Big Buddha statues in Thailand began centuries ago, with the first recorded one built in Sukhothai during the 13th century. Since then, numerous statues have been erected across the country, each with its unique charm and history. These statues serve as a reminder of the country's spiritual heritage and provide a tranquil space for meditation and reflection.

Architectural Marvels :

The architecture of the Big Buddha statues is awe-inspiring and showcases the skill and craftsmanship of Thai artisans. The statues are typically crafted from durable materials such as marble, bronze, or concrete and are meticulously designed with intricate details and embellishments.

One of the most renowned Big Buddha statues in Thailand is the Phra Buddha Chinnarat in Phitsanulok. Dating back to the 14th century, this statue features a stunning blend of Sukhothai and Lanna styles, with its graceful posture and serene facial expression captivating visitors. Another notable statue is the Big Buddha of Wat Muang in Ang Thong, standing at an impressive height of 92 meters, making it one of the tallest Buddha statues in the world.

Top Big Buddha Destinations in Thailand :

a. Wat Phra That Doi Suthep, Chiang Mai:

Situated atop Doi Suthep Mountain, the Big Buddha at Wat Phra That Doi Suthep is a prominent attraction in Chiang Mai. Visitors can ascend the mountain via a scenic road or choose to climb the 309 steps of the Naga staircase, which is adorned with intricate serpent-like creatures. Upon reaching the top, they are rewarded with breathtaking panoramic views of the city and a magnificent golden Big Buddha statue.

b. Big Buddha, Phuket:

Perched atop Nakkerd Hill, the Big Buddha in Phuket is a remarkable sight that dominates the island's skyline. Standing at 45 meters tall, it is one of the island's most significant landmarks. Visitors can explore the site, learn about Buddhist teachings, and enjoy panoramic vistas of the surrounding beaches and lush landscapes.

c. Wat Muang, Ang Thong:
Located in the province of Ang Thong, Wat Muang is home to the colossal Big Buddha statue, which is truly a sight to behold. Visitors can climb the staircase leading to the base of the statue, gaining a sense of the statue's immense scale and the intricate details carved into its surface. The surrounding temple complex also offers insight into Thai religious and cultural practices.

d. Big Buddha, Pattaya:
Situated on Pratumnak Hill in Pattaya, the Big Buddha here offers a tranquil escape from the city's bustling atmosphere. This relatively newer addition to Thailand's Big Buddha collection still manages to impress visitors with its serene ambiance and stunning views of the Gulf of Thailand. The site also features beautifully manicured gardens and a meditation area for contemplation.

e. Phra Buddha Maha Nawamin, Ang Thong:
The grandest Big Buddha statue in Thailand, Phra Buddha Maha Nawamin, is located in the province of Ang Thong. Standing at a

staggering height of 92 meters, this statue is an engineering marvel. Visitors can explore the base, which houses a museum showcasing Buddhist artifacts and offers a panoramic elevator ride to an observation deck for sweeping views of the countryside.

Immersive Experiences and Cultural Insights :

Visiting the Big Buddha statues in Thailand offers more than just visual splendor. It provides an opportunity to immerse oneself in Thai culture, gain spiritual insights, and participate in religious practices. Many of the Big Buddha sites have meditation areas or offer meditation retreats where visitors can learn and practice mindfulness under the guidance of experienced monks.

Furthermore, visitors can witness and partake in traditional ceremonies and rituals that take place at the Big Buddha sites. These include lighting incense, making offerings, and joining in prayer, which allows for a deeper understanding of Thai Buddhism and its significance in local life.

Practical Information and Tips :

a. Best Time to Visit: The Big Buddha sites can be visited year-round, but it is recommended to avoid peak tourist seasons for a more peaceful experience. The cooler months between November and February are ideal.

b. Dress Code and Etiquette: As these sites hold religious significance, it is essential to dress modestly and respectfully. Avoid wearing revealing clothing and remember to remove your shoes when entering temple areas.

c. Guided Tours: Consider joining guided tours or hiring a local guide to gain a better understanding of the cultural and historical significance of the Big Buddha sites.

d. Photography and Respect: While photography is generally allowed, be mindful of the surroundings and the locals' privacy. Avoid touching or climbing on the statues, and adhere to any posted rules or guidelines.

The Big Buddha statues in Thailand offer a profound and enriching experience for visitors. As icons of spirituality, they exemplify the deep-rooted Buddhist traditions that have shaped Thai society. A visit to these majestic statues provides an opportunity for cultural immersion, spiritual contemplation, and a glimpse into the architectural marvels of Thailand. Incorporate a journey to the Big

Buddha sites into your travel itinerary to embark on a transformative adventure that embraces the heart and soul of Thailand.

Phang Nga Bay

Nestled along Thailand's Andaman Sea coast, Phang Nga Bay is an enchanting destination that captivates visitors with its natural beauty, stunning limestone karsts, emerald waters, and diverse marine life. This hidden gem has gained recognition as one of the top tourist destinations in Thailand, offering a unique blend of breathtaking landscapes, outdoor adventures, cultural experiences, and tranquility. In this comprehensive Thailand travel guide, we will explore the allure of Phang Nga Bay, its key attractions, activities, cultural highlights, and practical tips to help you make the most of your visit.

Geographical Overview:

Phang Nga Bay is located in the province of Phang Nga, just north of Phuket, one of Thailand's most popular tourist destinations.

The bay covers an expansive area of approximately 400 square kilometers, characterized by limestone cliffs rising dramatically from the clear turquoise waters. The bay comprises numerous islands, including the famous James Bond Island (Khao Phing Kan), which gained global recognition after featuring in the 1974 James Bond movie "The Man with the Golden Gun."

Natural Wonders and Landscapes:

Phang Nga Bay's breathtaking natural landscapes are its main draw. The towering limestone karsts, often covered in lush greenery, create a surreal atmosphere and offer countless photo opportunities. These stunning geological formations are the result of millions of years of erosion, making Phang Nga Bay a geological marvel worth exploring. The bay is also home to hidden lagoons, mysterious caves, and secluded beaches, which can be discovered by kayak or traditional longtail boat.

Iconic Attractions:
a. James Bond Island (Khao Phing Kan): As mentioned earlier, this iconic island gained international fame after appearing in a James Bond film. It features a distinctive limestone

rock formation jutting out of the water, offering a picturesque and Instagram-worthy sight.

b. Koh Panyee: A floating village built on stilts, Koh Panyee is an extraordinary community that showcases the resilience and adaptability of its inhabitants. Visitors can explore the village, enjoy fresh seafood, and observe the local way of life.

c. Hong Island: Accessible only by boat, Hong Island boasts mesmerizing turquoise waters, pristine beaches, and hidden lagoons. Snorkeling, swimming, and picnicking in this secluded paradise are must-do activities.

d. Koh Tapu: Known as the Nail Island or the Spike Island, Koh Tapu is another fascinating limestone rock formation rising dramatically from the sea. It offers a surreal backdrop for exploring the surrounding waters and beaches.

Outdoor Adventures:
Phang Nga Bay provides a plethora of outdoor activities for adventure enthusiasts:
a. Kayaking: Exploring the hidden lagoons, mangrove forests, and caves by kayak is an exhilarating experience that allows you to get

up close and personal with the bay's unique flora and fauna.

b. Scuba Diving and Snorkeling: The bay's crystal-clear waters host vibrant coral reefs, colorful marine life, and hidden underwater caves. Snorkeling and scuba diving tours offer an unforgettable glimpse into this marine wonderland.

c. Rock Climbing: The limestone cliffs of Phang Nga Bay provide an excellent backdrop for rock climbing adventures. Climbing enthusiasts of all levels can test their skills and enjoy breathtaking views from the top.

d. Hiking and Trekking: The surrounding forests and hills offer excellent opportunities for hiking and trekking, with trails leading to viewpoints that offer panoramic vistas of the bay and its surroundings.

Cultural Experiences:
Phang Nga Bay is not only renowned for its natural beauty but also for its rich cultural heritage. Visitors can immerse themselves in the local culture through the following experiences:
a. Visiting Buddhist Temples: Explore the sacred Wat Suwan Khuha Temple, also known

as the "Cave Temple," which houses a large reclining Buddha statue. This temple holds great spiritual significance for the locals.

b. Learning Traditional Fishing Techniques: Engage with the local fishing communities and gain insights into their traditional fishing techniques, such as crab trapping and net casting. It's a unique opportunity to connect with the local way of life.

c. Sampling Local Cuisine: Indulge in the authentic flavors of southern Thai cuisine, which showcases a diverse range of dishes with a blend of spicy, sweet, and savory flavors. Don't miss out on the region's fresh seafood delicacies.

Practical Tips for Visitors:

a. Best Time to Visit: The ideal time to visit Phang Nga Bay is during the dry season, which extends from November to April, offering pleasant weather and calm seas. The monsoon season, from May to October, brings heavier rainfall and rougher waters.

b. Getting There: Phang Nga Bay is easily accessible from Phuket, which has an international airport. Visitors can take a short boat ride from Phuket or Krabi to reach the bay's key attractions.

c. Choosing Accommodation: Accommodation options range from luxury resorts and boutique hotels to budget-friendly guesthouses. It's recommended to stay in Phuket or Krabi and take day trips to explore Phang Nga Bay.

d. Respect the Environment: As a responsible traveler, it's important to respect the fragile ecosystem of Phang Nga Bay. Avoid littering, follow designated trails, and adhere to guidelines for wildlife encounters to preserve this pristine natural wonder.

Phang Nga Bay has rightfully earned its place as a top tourist destination in Thailand. Its awe-inspiring landscapes, captivating attractions, and opportunities for outdoor adventures and cultural immersion make it a must-visit for travelers seeking a unique and unforgettable experience. Whether you're kayaking through hidden lagoons, exploring mysterious caves, or simply admiring the breathtaking scenery, Phang Nga Bay promises an enchanting journey that will leave you with memories to cherish for a lifetime.

•Krabi

Nestled on the picturesque Andaman Sea coast, Krabi is a tropical paradise that lures travelers from all corners of the world. With its stunning natural landscapes, pristine beaches, crystal-clear waters, and limestone cliffs, Krabi has established itself as one of Thailand's top tourist destinations. This comprehensive travel guide will delve into the enchanting allure of Krabi, exploring its captivating attractions, vibrant culture, thrilling activities, and enticing culinary delights, ensuring that your visit to this coastal gem is truly unforgettable.

Geographical Overview

Located on the southwestern coast of Thailand, Krabi is part of the Krabi Province and is situated approximately 800 kilometers south of Bangkok. Its strategic location provides easy access to a multitude of islands and national parks, making it a haven for nature lovers and adventure seekers alike. Krabi boasts an extensive coastline dotted with numerous beaches, each offering its unique charm and character.

Krabi's Natural Splendor

2.1 Pristine Beaches

Krabi is renowned for its pristine beaches, which rank among some of the most beautiful in the world. The iconic Railay Beach, accessible only by boat due to the towering limestone cliffs that surround it, is a paradise for rock climbers and beach lovers. Other popular beaches include Ao Nang, Klong Muang, and Nopparat Thara Beach, each boasting soft sands, turquoise waters, and a range of water sports and beachside activities.

2.2 Majestic Islands

A visit to Krabi is incomplete without exploring its breathtaking islands. The Phi Phi Islands, composed of Phi Phi Don and Phi Phi Leh, are a highlight for travelers. With their emerald-green waters, vibrant coral reefs, and towering cliffs, these islands offer extraordinary opportunities for snorkeling, diving, and island-hopping adventures. Other notable islands include the Hong Islands, Chicken Island, and the Four Islands, each showcasing their unique natural wonders.

2.3 Striking Limestone Cliffs

Krabi's distinct feature is its dramatic limestone cliffs, which stand tall and majestic throughout the region. These towering karsts provide a stunning backdrop to the beaches and offer adventurous activities such as rock climbing, hiking, and cave exploration. One of the most famous limestone formations is Khao Khanab Nam, located near the city center, offering a fascinating insight into the region's geological wonders.

2.4 Pristine National Parks

Krabi is also home to several national parks, each offering a diverse range of ecosystems and natural beauty. The Hat Noppharat Thara-Mu Ko Phi Phi National Park, with its marine-rich waters, vibrant coral reefs, and lush forests, is a paradise for nature enthusiasts. Another notable park is Than Bok Khorani National Park, boasting stunning waterfalls, limestone caves, and tranquil nature trails, providing an excellent opportunity for hiking and wildlife spotting.

Cultural Delights
3.1 Krabi Town

Krabi Town, the provincial capital, offers a glimpse into the local culture and lifestyle. With its bustling markets, charming riverside walkways, and vibrant night markets, the town provides a lively atmosphere for travelers to immerse themselves in the local customs. The Krabi Town Walking Street, held every weekend, is a must-visit, offering a variety of local street food, handicrafts, and live performances.

3.2 Temples and Shrines

Krabi is dotted with numerous temples and shrines that reflect the region's deep-rooted spiritual beliefs. The Wat Tham Sua (Tiger Cave Temple) is a significant religious site that offers panoramic views of Krabi from its summit, but it requires climbing 1,237 steps. Other notable temples include Wat Kaew Korawaram and Wat Klong Thom Museum, each showcasing distinctive architectural styles and rich historical significance.

Thrilling Activities
4.1 Rock Climbing

With its towering limestone cliffs, Krabi has gained international acclaim as a premier rock climbing destination. Whether you're a beginner or an experienced climber, Railay Beach and Tonsai Beach offer a wide range of climbing routes suitable for all skill levels. Expert instructors and climbing schools are readily available, ensuring a safe and exhilarating experience for all adventure enthusiasts.

4.2 Scuba Diving and Snorkeling

The crystal-clear waters surrounding Krabi are teeming with vibrant marine life and stunning coral reefs, making it a haven for scuba diving and snorkeling. Dive sites such as Hin Daeng, Hin Muang, and the Phi Phi Islands offer incredible underwater experiences, with encounters with turtles, reef sharks, and colorful tropical fish. Snorkeling trips to popular spots like Bamboo Island and the Four Islands are also widely available, allowing visitors to explore the captivating underwater world.

4.3 Sea Kayaking

Exploring Krabi's hidden lagoons, mangrove forests, and secluded caves by sea kayak is an adventure not to be missed. The mangrove maze of Ao Thalane is a popular kayaking destination, where paddling through narrow channels and witnessing the diverse flora and fauna is a unique and serene experience. Guided tours and sunset kayaking trips provide ample opportunities to soak in the natural beauty of Krabi's coast.

Gastronomic Delights

Krabi offers a diverse culinary scene that caters to all taste buds. From fresh seafood delicacies to authentic Thai street food, the region presents a gastronomic adventure for food enthusiasts. Night markets such as the Krabi Town Walking Street and the Ao Nang Market offer a vibrant array of local dishes, including Pad Thai, green curry, Tom Yum soup, and the famous mango sticky rice. For those seeking a romantic dining experience, beachside restaurants and seafood barbecues under the starlit sky are a perfect choice.

Krabi, with its natural splendor, vibrant culture, and thrilling activities, stands as a top tourist destination in Thailand. Whether you seek a relaxing beach getaway, an adrenaline-filled adventure, or a cultural immersion, Krabi offers an experience that caters to every traveler's desires. With its stunning beaches, majestic limestone cliffs, enchanting islands, and warm hospitality, Krabi invites you to embark on an unforgettable journey into the heart of paradise.

Railay Beach

Thailand, a Southeast Asian gem, is known for its stunning beaches, rich culture, and vibrant cities. Among its many beautiful coastal destinations, Railay Beach stands out as a top tourist hotspot. Located in the Krabi Province, Railay Beach offers visitors a truly unforgettable experience with its breathtaking scenery, crystal-clear waters, and a range of exciting activities. This Thailand travel guide will delve into the enchanting world of Railay Beach, exploring its natural wonders, recreational opportunities, accommodation options, and cultural highlights. Get ready to embark on an extraordinary adventure to one of Thailand's most sought-after destinations.

Natural Beauty

Railay Beach is renowned for its unparalleled natural beauty, captivating travelers with its picturesque landscapes and pristine surroundings. Nestled between towering limestone cliffs and surrounded by lush tropical greenery, the beach exudes a tranquil ambiance that is perfect for relaxation and rejuvenation. The stunning turquoise waters of the Andaman Sea offer a refreshing escape from the hustle and bustle of everyday life, making Railay Beach an ideal destination for beach lovers and nature enthusiasts.

Activities and Adventures

Railay Beach offers an array of activities and adventures to suit every traveler's interests. Rock climbing enthusiasts flock to the cliffs that surround the beach, as Railay is considered one of the top rock climbing destinations in the world. Whether you're a seasoned climber or a beginner looking to try something new, Railay's limestone karsts provide an exhilarating challenge for climbers of all skill levels.

For those seeking underwater exploration, Railay Beach offers excellent diving and snorkeling opportunities. Dive into the clear waters to discover vibrant coral reefs, colorful marine life, and even the chance to swim with majestic sea turtles. Kayaking and paddleboarding are also popular activities, allowing visitors to explore the coastline and hidden lagoons at their own pace.

Pristine Beaches
Railay Beach is actually divided into four distinct sections: Railay West, Railay East, Phra Nang Cave Beach, and Tonsai Beach. Each of these beaches has its own unique charm and appeal. Railay West is the main beach, known for its stunning sunsets and powdery white sand. The calm waters here are perfect for swimming and sunbathing.

On the eastern side of the peninsula, Railay East offers a more budget-friendly accommodation option and a lively nightlife scene. Travelers can enjoy beachside bars, live music, and a variety of restaurants serving both local and international cuisine.

Phra Nang Cave Beach, named after the revered Princess Cave located there, is considered one of the most beautiful beaches in the world. With its crystal-clear waters, towering limestone cliffs, and fine sand, this beach is a true tropical paradise. Tonsai Beach, on the other hand, is popular among backpackers and rock climbers, offering a more rustic and laid-back atmosphere.

Accommodation Options
Railay Beach caters to all types of travelers with its diverse range of accommodation options. From luxury resorts to budget-friendly bungalows, there is something to suit every preference and budget. For those seeking a luxurious experience, there are several high-end resorts that offer stunning views, private pools, and world-class amenities.

On the other hand, budget-conscious travelers can find affordable guesthouses and bungalows that provide basic yet comfortable accommodations. Many of these options are located just a short walk from the beach, making them convenient for travelers looking to maximize their time in the sun and sand.

Local Cuisine and Culture
Thailand is renowned for its delicious cuisine, and Railay Beach is no exception. Visitors can indulge in a wide range of culinary delights, from fresh seafood barbecues to traditional Thai dishes bursting with flavor. Numerous

beachside restaurants and cafes offer an extensive menu of local and international dishes, ensuring there is something to satisfy every palate.

Railay Beach also provides an opportunity to immerse oneself in the local culture. Explore the nearby Krabi Town, where you can visit bustling markets, ancient temples, and experience the warm hospitality of the Thai people. Take part in traditional Thai cooking classes, where you can learn to prepare authentic dishes using fresh local ingredients. Additionally, don't miss the chance to witness a traditional Thai dance performance, a captivating display of graceful movements and vibrant costumes.

Railay Beach is undeniably one of Thailand's top tourist destinations, offering visitors a perfect blend of natural beauty, thrilling activities, and cultural experiences. Whether you're seeking a relaxing beach getaway, an adrenaline-fueled adventure, or an opportunity to immerse yourself in Thai culture, Railay Beach has it all. From its breathtaking scenery and pristine beaches to its diverse range of accommodation options and delectable cuisine, this tropical paradise is a must-visit destination for anyone traveling to Thailand. Embark on a journey to Railay Beach and create memories that will last a lifetime.

Koh Phi Phi

Thailand is renowned for its breathtaking natural beauty, vibrant culture, and world-class tourist destinations. Among these gems is Koh Phi Phi, an archipelago located in the Andaman Sea, which has gained fame as a must-visit destination for travelers around the globe. With its stunning beaches, crystal-clear waters, lush greenery, and vibrant nightlife, Koh Phi Phi offers an unforgettable experience that truly captures the essence of a tropical paradise. In this Thailand travel guide, we will delve into the enchanting allure of Koh Phi Phi, exploring its rich history, natural wonders, exciting activities, and practical travel tips that will help you make the most of your visit to this top tourist destination.

A Brief History of Koh Phi Phi
To truly appreciate the beauty of Koh Phi Phi, it is important to understand its historical

significance. The archipelago has a fascinating past that dates back centuries. Originally inhabited by sea gypsies, Koh Phi Phi later became a thriving trading hub during the late 18th century. However, in 2004, the region was tragically devastated by the Indian Ocean tsunami, causing significant damage to the island. Despite this setback, the resilient spirit of the locals, along with the support of the Thai government and international aid, led to the successful reconstruction and revival of Koh Phi Phi as a top tourist destination.

Natural Wonders and Breathtaking Beaches

Koh Phi Phi boasts an abundance of natural wonders that will leave visitors awestruck. The archipelago is characterized by towering limestone cliffs, hidden lagoons, and emerald-green waters teeming with vibrant marine life. Maya Bay, located on the uninhabited Phi Phi Leh Island, gained international fame as the setting for the movie "The Beach," starring Leonardo DiCaprio. Although temporarily closed for ecological restoration, the bay's stunning beauty can still be appreciated from the surrounding viewpoints. Another must-visit beach is Long Beach, offering a serene atmosphere and pristine white sand. Other notable beaches include Loh Dalum Bay, Ton Sai Bay, and Monkey Beach, each offering unique features and opportunities for relaxation and water activities.

Diving and Snorkeling in Koh Phi Phi
The underwater world surrounding Koh Phi Phi is a playground for divers and snorkelers. With crystal-clear waters and thriving coral reefs, the archipelago offers exceptional diving opportunities. Hin Muang and Hin Daeng are renowned dive sites where divers can explore vibrant coral gardens and encounter exotic marine species, including manta rays and whale sharks. For those new to diving, numerous diving schools and instructors are available on the island, providing lessons and certification courses. Snorkeling enthusiasts can also enjoy the wonders of the underwater world, as many tour operators offer snorkeling trips to popular spots such as Bamboo Island and Mosquito Island, where colorful coral and tropical fish abound.

Exploring the Surrounding Islands
Koh Phi Phi serves as an excellent base for exploring the nearby islands, each with its own distinct charm. Bamboo Island, located just a

short boat ride away, offers pristine beaches, crystal-clear waters, and excellent snorkeling opportunities. Phi Phi Leh Island, despite the closure of Maya Bay, is worth a visit for its stunning cliffs, hidden lagoons, and the iconic Viking Cave. The nearby Phang Nga Bay, with its towering limestone karsts and floating villages, is another popular destination that can be easily reached from Koh Phi Phi.

Vibrant Nightlife and Entertainment

When the sun sets, Koh Phi Phi comes alive with its vibrant nightlife and entertainment options. The island's main hub, Tonsai Village, is lined with bustling bars, nightclubs, and restaurants, offering a lively atmosphere that caters to all tastes. Fire shows, live music performances, and beach parties are common occurrences, creating a festive ambiance that attracts partygoers from all over the world. For those seeking a more relaxed evening, there are also quieter beachfront venues where you can unwind and enjoy the gentle sound of the waves under the starlit sky.

Practical Tips for Visiting Koh Phi Phi

To make the most of your trip to Koh Phi Phi, here are some practical tips to keep in mind. Firstly, the best time to visit is during the dry season, from November to April, when the weather is most favorable for outdoor activities. It is advisable to book accommodation in advance, especially during peak seasons, to ensure availability and secure the best rates. When exploring the islands, be sure to bring essentials such as sunscreen, mosquito repellent, and appropriate footwear for hiking and water activities. Additionally, it is important to respect the local culture and environment by avoiding littering and adhering to responsible tourism practices.

Koh Phi Phi is undeniably a top tourist destination in Thailand, offering a paradise-like experience that captivates the hearts of travelers. With its stunning natural beauty, pristine beaches, diverse marine life, exciting activities, and vibrant nightlife, it's no wonder that visitors from around the world flock to this enchanting archipelago. Whether you seek relaxation on the beach, exhilaration beneath the waves, or a lively party scene, Koh Phi Phi has something to offer every type of traveler. So pack your bags, prepare for an unforgettable adventure, and immerse yourself in the captivating allure of Koh Phi Phi, a tropical paradise like no other.

Tiger Cave Temple

Thailand, known for its captivating landscapes and rich cultural heritage, offers a multitude of attractions for travelers seeking an immersive experience. Amidst the countless gems, the Tiger Cave Temple stands out as a must-visit destination. Located in Krabi province, this iconic Buddhist temple, also known as Wat Tham Sua, has gained fame for its stunning natural surroundings, spiritual significance, and challenging hike. In this comprehensive Thailand travel guide, we will delve into the allure of Tiger Cave Temple, highlighting its historical and cultural significance, providing practical travel tips, and inviting you to embark on an unforgettable journey of self-discovery.

I. Historical and Cultural Significance
A. Origins and Legend

The Tiger Cave Temple holds deep roots in Thai history, dating back over 2,000 years. Legend has it that a wandering monk discovered a tiger living within a cave, hence the temple's name. Fascinated by the natural beauty and solitude of the area, the monk decided to establish a place of worship, marking the birth of this sacred site.

B. Buddhist Heritage
Tiger Cave Temple is renowned as a prominent Buddhist center in Southern Thailand. It is home to several monks who have dedicated their lives to practicing meditation and promoting Buddhist teachings. The temple complex encompasses numerous shrines, statues, and meditation caves, making it an ideal spot for those seeking spiritual enlightenment or a tranquil retreat.

II. Exploring the Temple Complex
A. The Grand Pagoda
The centerpiece of Tiger Cave Temple is the grand pagoda, soaring high at 278 meters. Climbing the 1,237 steps to reach the pagoda is a challenging endeavor, but the panoramic views of Krabi's lush landscapes and the Andaman Sea make it all worthwhile. At the peak, visitors are greeted by a golden Buddha statue and a serene ambiance that instills a sense of peace and awe.

B. Meditation Caves
The temple complex encompasses several meditation caves, each offering a unique

atmosphere for introspection and self-reflection. The caves are adorned with intricate Buddhist carvings and provide a serene environment for visitors to experience a moment of tranquility amidst the bustling world outside.

C. Monastic Life

Exploring Tiger Cave Temple offers an opportunity to witness the daily routines of Buddhist monks. Visitors can observe morning alms-giving ceremonies or even participate in meditation sessions guided by experienced practitioners. Engaging with the monks can provide valuable insights into Thai Buddhism and foster a deeper understanding of their way of life.

III. Natural Wonders Surrounding the Temple

A. The Forest Reserve

Tiger Cave Temple is situated within a lush forest reserve, offering a haven for nature enthusiasts. The area boasts diverse flora and fauna, including rare plant species and exotic wildlife. Exploring the surrounding trails allows visitors to immerse themselves in the enchanting beauty of the tropical rainforest, providing a refreshing break from the urban hustle and bustle.

B. Khiriwong Valley
Adjacent to Tiger Cave Temple lies Khiriwong Valley, a picturesque village known for its stunning landscapes and traditional way of life. Embark on a short excursion from the temple to experience the rustic charm of the village, interact with the locals, and savor authentic Thai cuisine.

IV. Practical Travel Tips
A. Best Time to Visit
The ideal time to visit Tiger Cave Temple is during the dry season, between November and April. The weather is pleasant, with moderate temperatures and low chances of rainfall. It is advisable to avoid weekends and public holidays, as the temple tends to be crowded with tourists during these times.

B. Dress Code and Etiquette
As a place of worship, it is essential to dress modestly and respectfully when visiting the temple. Both men and women should ensure their shoulders and knees are covered. Additionally, visitors are advised to maintain a quiet demeanor, refrain from touching sacred

objects without permission, and remove their shoes when entering temples or meditation caves.

C. Physical Fitness and Safety Precautions
Ascending the stairs to the grand pagoda requires a reasonable level of physical fitness. It is advisable to wear comfortable shoes, carry sufficient water, and take breaks whenever necessary. Visitors with medical conditions or physical limitations should consult their healthcare provider before attempting the climb.

Tiger Cave Temple stands as a testament to Thailand's cultural richness and natural beauty. Its unique combination of spiritual significance, breathtaking views, and the harmony between man and nature makes it a top tourist destination in Thailand. As you embark on your journey to this enchanting temple, embrace the tranquility, immerse yourself in the history, and let the spirituality of the Tiger Cave Temple captivate your senses.

Four Islands Tour

Thailand is renowned for its stunning natural beauty, pristine beaches, and vibrant culture. Among its many attractions, the Four Islands Tour stands out as one of the most sought-after experiences for travelers. This extraordinary journey takes visitors on an unforgettable adventure through four exquisite islands in the Andaman Sea: Koh Phi Phi, Koh Lanta, Koh Ngai, and Koh Mook. In this comprehensive Thailand travel guide, we will delve into the captivating allure of the Four Islands Tour, highlighting its breathtaking landscapes, exciting activities, and the cultural gems that await visitors.

Koh Phi Phi: The Jewel of the Andaman Sea

Koh Phi Phi, often regarded as the crown jewel of the Andaman Sea, is the first stop on the Four Islands Tour. This magnificent archipelago consists of two main islands: Koh Phi Phi Don and Koh Phi Phi Leh. The crystal-clear turquoise waters, towering limestone cliffs, and vibrant marine life make it a paradise for nature lovers and adventure enthusiasts.

a. Maya Bay: Immortalized by Hollywood

Maya Bay, located on Koh Phi Phi Leh, gained worldwide fame after it was featured in the movie "The Beach." Enclosed by towering cliffs and boasting pristine white sands, this secluded bay offers a picturesque setting for swimming, snorkeling, and sunbathing.

b. Phi Phi Viewpoint: A Panoramic Delight
For breathtaking views of the archipelago, a hike to the Phi Phi Viewpoint is a must. The challenging trek uphill rewards visitors with panoramic vistas of the surrounding islands, azure waters, and lush greenery.

c. Monkey Beach: Up Close with Nature's Playful Residents
Monkey Beach, situated on Koh Phi Phi Don, provides an opportunity to interact with playful macaques in their natural habitat. Visitors can also enjoy snorkeling amidst colorful coral reefs, surrounded by a vibrant array of tropical fish.

Koh Lanta: Serenity and Scenic Splendor
The next stop on the Four Islands Tour is Koh Lanta, a tranquil island known for its serene atmosphere and captivating beauty. With its long stretches of sandy beaches, lush

rainforests, and warm hospitality, Koh Lanta offers a relaxing escape from the bustling tourist hubs.

a. Long Beach: Relaxation Personified

Long Beach, stretching along the west coast of Koh Lanta, is a paradise for beach lovers seeking tranquility. Its soft sands, clear waters, and mesmerizing sunsets create an idyllic ambiance for sunbathing, swimming, or simply unwinding with a book.

b. Mu Ko Lanta National Park: Exploring Nature's Wonders

Nature enthusiasts should not miss a visit to Mu Ko Lanta National Park. With its dense mangrove forests, diverse wildlife, and pristine coral reefs, this park offers opportunities for hiking, snorkeling, and wildlife spotting. The picturesque Lanta Lighthouse, perched atop a hill, provides panoramic views of the island and its surroundings.

Koh Ngai: An Undiscovered Gem

Koh Ngai, also known as Koh Hai, is a hidden gem that exudes tranquility and charm. Its unspoiled beaches, swaying palm trees, and crystal-clear waters offer an intimate and secluded experience for travelers seeking an off-the-beaten-path paradise.

a. Paradise Lost: Exploring Emerald Cave
One of the highlights of Koh Ngai is the Emerald Cave, a natural wonder accessible only by swimming through a dark tunnel. Inside, visitors are rewarded with a hidden lagoon surrounded by towering cliffs and a vibrant emerald glow, creating a surreal experience.

b. Snorkeling and Diving: Underwater Marvels
Koh Ngai's coral reefs are teeming with a kaleidoscope of marine life. Snorkeling or diving in the azure waters reveals a captivating world of colorful corals, tropical fish, and even sea turtles, making it a haven for underwater enthusiasts.

Koh Mook: An Enchanting Hideaway
The final stop on the Four Islands Tour is Koh Mook, a captivating island known for its pristine beaches, lush vegetation, and welcoming local communities. This unspoiled paradise offers a glimpse into authentic Thai island life.
a. Tham Morakot (Emerald Cave): Nature's Hidden Gem
Similar to the Emerald Cave on Koh Ngai, Tham Morakot, also known as the Emerald Cave on Koh Mook, promises an awe-inspiring adventure. Visitors can swim through a

dramatic cave passage, emerging in a secluded beach enclosed by towering cliffs and vibrant greenery.

b. Fishing Village and Local Culture
Exploring the fishing village on Koh Mook provides a unique opportunity to connect with the local community and experience their traditional way of life. Engage in conversations with friendly fishermen, sample delicious seafood, and witness the vibrant culture that thrives on the island.

The Four Islands Tour is a remarkable opportunity to explore the mesmerizing beauty of Thailand's Andaman Sea. From the iconic limestone cliffs of Koh Phi Phi to the serene beaches of Koh Lanta, the hidden treasures of Koh Ngai, and the enchanting allure of Koh Mook, this adventure promises an unforgettable experience for travelers seeking natural splendor and cultural immersion. Embrace the magic of these four islands and create memories that will last a lifetime on this top tourist destination in Thailand.

CHAPTER FOUR

Cultural Experiences and Festivals

•*Thai Cuisine and Street Food*

Thailand, a country known for its vibrant culture, stunning landscapes, and warm hospitality, has also earned a reputation as a top destination for food lovers. Thai cuisine is celebrated worldwide for its rich flavors, aromatic herbs, and bold spices. From exquisite fine dining establishments to humble street food stalls, Thailand offers a diverse culinary experience that caters to every palate. In this travel guide, we delve into the enchanting world of Thai cuisine and street food, exploring the must-try dishes, popular food markets, and tips for an unforgettable gastronomic journey.

Thai Cuisine: A Fusion of Flavors

Thai cuisine is a harmonious blend of influences from neighboring countries such as China, India, and Malaysia, combined with its unique culinary traditions. The balance of sweet, sour, salty, and spicy flavors is a hallmark of Thai dishes. From the world-renowned Pad Thai to the aromatic Green Curry, the variety and depth of Thai cuisine are truly remarkable. The use of fresh ingredients like lemongrass, kaffir lime leaves, Thai basil, and galangal infuses the dishes with distinct flavors that awaken the senses.

Street Food Culture in Thailand:
Thai street food is an integral part of the local culinary scene. The streets of Bangkok, Chiang Mai, and other cities are transformed into bustling food havens as dusk falls. Night markets and street food stalls line the streets, offering a mouthwatering array of dishes. Thai street food is not only delicious but also affordable, making it a popular choice among locals and tourists alike. From fragrant noodle soups and grilled skewers to crispy fried insects and tropical fruit shakes, the choices are endless.

Exploring Bangkok's Street Food:
Bangkok, the capital city of Thailand, is a haven for food enthusiasts. The vibrant streets of Bangkok offer an overwhelming variety of street food options. The legendary street food

hub, Yaowarat (Chinatown), is a treasure trove of flavors where visitors can indulge in dishes like Hainanese chicken rice, crispy pork belly, and fresh seafood. Other notable street food destinations in Bangkok include Ratchawat Market, Khao San Road, and the famous floating markets where visitors can savor grilled river prawns and traditional boat noodles.

Chiang Mai's Street Food Delights:
Chiang Mai, the cultural heart of northern Thailand, is renowned for its unique street food scene. The city's night bazaars, such as the Sunday Walking Street and the Chiang Mai Night Bazaar, come alive with the aroma of freshly cooked delicacies. The region's signature dish, Khao Soi, a flavorful curry noodle soup, is a must-try. Visitors can also enjoy dishes like Sai Oua (northern Thai sausage), Khanom Krok (coconut rice pancakes), and various stir-fried delicacies.

Regional Specialties:
Thailand's culinary delights are not limited to its major cities. Each region has its own distinctive dishes that reflect the local ingredients and culinary traditions. In the coastal areas of Southern Thailand, seafood

dishes like Tom Yam Talay (spicy seafood soup) and Pla Rad Prik (fried fish with chili sauce) take center stage. In the northeastern region, known as Isan, visitors can savor dishes like Som Tum (green papaya salad) and Larb (spicy minced meat salad). Exploring these regional specialties provides a deeper understanding of the diverse culinary landscape of Thailand.

Food Markets and Cooking Classes:
Visiting food markets in Thailand offers a unique cultural experience. Markets such as Chatuchak Weekend Market in Bangkok and Warorot Market in Chiang Mai are not only bustling with fresh produce and local ingredients but also offer a wide range of street food options. Additionally, many culinary schools and cooking classes in Thailand provide visitors with an opportunity to learn the art of Thai cooking, allowing them to recreate the flavors of Thailand in their own kitchens.

Tips for Enjoying Thai Cuisine and Street Food:
To make the most of your culinary adventure in Thailand, here are some tips:

a) Hygiene: Look for clean and busy food stalls to ensure food safety.

b) Experiment: Be adventurous and try dishes you've never had before.

c) Spice Level: Thai food can be spicy, so communicate your preferred spice level to the vendor.

d) Thai Etiquette: Use a spoon and fork for eating, and remember to sample a variety of dishes and share them with your companions.

Thailand's cuisine and street food culture offer an unforgettable culinary adventure. Exploring the diverse flavors, vibrant markets, and iconic dishes of Thai cuisine is an essential part of any visit to this remarkable country. Whether you're strolling through the bustling streets of Bangkok or exploring the charming markets of Chiang Mai, Thailand's culinary delights will leave you craving for more. Immerse yourself in the gastronomic wonders of Thailand and savor the exquisite flavors that make this country a top destination for food lovers around the world.

•Muay Thai Boxing

Thailand, known as the "Land of Smiles," is a country renowned for its rich culture, vibrant history, breathtaking landscapes, and warm hospitality. Among the many attractions that draw travelers from all corners of the globe, Muay Thai Boxing stands out as a unique and thrilling experience. With its origins deeply rooted in Thai culture and history, Muay Thai has evolved into a global phenomenon, captivating both locals and tourists alike. In this travel guide, we will explore the fascinating world of Muay Thai Boxing and why it has become a must-visit destination for travelers seeking an authentic Thai experience.

A Brief History of Muay Thai:

Muay Thai, also known as Thai Boxing, is a martial art and combat sport that originated in Thailand centuries ago. It traces its roots back to the times of the ancient Siamese warriors who developed this form of combat for self-defense and warfare. Over time, Muay Thai evolved into a sport and an integral part of Thai culture, with bouts being held during festivals and celebrations. Today, it has gained international recognition and has become one of the most popular martial arts in the world.

The Cultural Significance of Muay Thai:
Muay Thai is not just a sport; it holds deep cultural significance in Thailand. It embodies the Thai values of discipline, respect, and perseverance. The rituals and traditions associated with Muay Thai, such as the Wai Kru Ram Muay (a pre-fight dance), showcase the respect and homage paid to the trainers, the sport, and the country's heritage. By witnessing and participating in these rituals, travelers gain a profound insight into Thai traditions and values, making their visit to Thailand truly memorable.

Top Muay Thai Training Camps:
Thailand is home to numerous Muay Thai training camps, where both professional fighters and enthusiasts train rigorously. These camps offer a unique opportunity for travelers to immerse themselves in the world of Muay Thai. Some of the top training camps in Thailand include Tiger Muay Thai in Phuket, Sitmonchai Gym in Kanchanaburi, and Fairtex Training Center in Pattaya. These camps provide world-class facilities, expert trainers, and a range of programs suitable for all skill

levels, from beginners to advanced practitioners.

Muay Thai Stadiums and Live Matches:
For an authentic Muay Thai experience, witnessing a live match in one of Thailand's renowned stadiums is a must. The excitement, energy, and skill displayed by the fighters, along with the cheering crowds, create an electrifying atmosphere. Bangkok's Rajadamnern Stadium and Lumpinee Stadium are two of the most prestigious venues where professional Muay Thai matches are held regularly. Travelers can witness the intensity of the fights, cheer for their favorite fighters, and appreciate the artistry and technique involved in this ancient martial art.

Muay Thai as a Fitness Activity:
Muay Thai's physical benefits have made it a popular fitness activity worldwide. Many training camps and gyms across Thailand offer Muay Thai classes for fitness enthusiasts of all levels. Engaging in Muay Thai training not only helps improve strength, endurance, and flexibility but also promotes weight loss and overall fitness. Taking part in these classes allows travelers to experience the physical

demands of Muay Thai while enjoying the tropical beauty of Thailand.

Muay Thai Retreats and Wellness Programs:

For those seeking a more holistic approach to Muay Thai, Thailand offers specialized retreats and wellness programs. These retreats combine Muay Thai training with yoga, meditation, and spa treatments, providing a well-rounded experience for the mind, body, and soul. These programs are often set in serene and picturesque locations, allowing travelers to rejuvenate and immerse themselves fully in the practice of Muay Thai while enjoying Thailand's natural beauty.

Muay Thai and Thai Cuisine:

No visit to Thailand is complete without savoring its world-famous cuisine. Muay Thai's close association with Thai culture is also reflected in the culinary realm. Many training camps and retreats offer healthy meal plans designed to complement the rigorous training routine. Travelers can indulge in delicious and nutritious Thai dishes, incorporating fresh ingredients, aromatic herbs, and the perfect balance of flavors. From mouthwatering curries to fragrant stir-fried dishes, Thai cuisine tantalizes the taste buds and offers a delightful culinary journey.

Muay Thai Souvenirs and Memorabilia:
For those looking to take a piece of Muay Thai home, Thailand offers a wide range of souvenirs and memorabilia. From traditional Muay Thai shorts and gloves to miniature figurines and decorative items, visitors can find a plethora of options to commemorate their experience. Local markets and specialty shops are the ideal places to hunt for these unique souvenirs, allowing travelers to cherish their memories of Muay Thai long after their visit.

Muay Thai Boxing has firmly established itself as a top tourist destination in Thailand. Its deep-rooted history, cultural significance, and thrilling nature make it an experience like no other. Whether it is training at world-class camps, witnessing live matches, embracing fitness through Muay Thai, or indulging in holistic retreats, Muay Thai offers an immersive journey into Thai culture and traditions. As travelers explore Thailand, engaging with Muay Thai allows them to understand the values of discipline, respect, and perseverance deeply ingrained in Thai society. Thus, for an unforgettable and authentic Thai experience, Muay Thai Boxing stands out as a must-visit destination in the Land of Smiles.

•*Loy Krathong Festival*

Thailand, a vibrant country known for its rich cultural heritage and captivating festivals, offers visitors an array of incredible experiences. Among these festivities, the Loy Krathong Festival stands out as a top tourist destination, drawing millions of visitors from around the globe each year. This captivating event, celebrated on the full moon night of the twelfth lunar month, showcases Thailand's devotion to spirituality and reverence for nature. In this comprehensive Thailand travel guide, we delve into the essence of the Loy Krathong Festival, its historical significance, mesmerizing rituals, and the best places to experience this awe-inspiring event. Prepare to embark on a journey of lights, colors, and enchantment as we explore the allure of Loy Krathong Festival in Thailand.

I. Historical Significance and Cultural Background :

The Loy Krathong Festival, also known as the Festival of Lights, has its roots deeply embedded in Thai history and culture. This ancient festival originated in the Sukhothai era, dating back to the 13th century. Loy Krathong was initially a Brahmanic festival that symbolized the paying of respects to the water goddess, Phra Mae Khongkha. Over time, the festival fused with Buddhist traditions, transforming into the captivating event celebrated today.

The word "Loy" means "to float," while "Krathong" refers to a small, lotus-shaped vessel made of banana leaves. These krathongs are traditionally decorated with flowers, candles, and incense sticks, and they are floated on rivers, canals, and lakes as an offering to the water spirits. The ritual signifies releasing negative energy and making wishes for a prosperous future.

II. The Enchanting Rituals of Loy Krathong :

Loy Krathong is renowned for its visually stunning rituals that captivate visitors and locals alike. The festival kicks off with a series of colorful parades featuring elaborately decorated floats, traditional music, and dance performances. These processions create a vibrant atmosphere, setting the stage for the main event.

As the sun sets, the rivers, canals, and lakes across Thailand come alive with flickering candlelight. Locals and tourists gather by the water's edge, lighting the candles and incense sticks on their krathongs before gently placing them onto the water. This magical sight creates a stunning tapestry of lights, as thousands of krathongs drift along the water, carrying with them people's hopes, dreams, and prayers.

In recent years, Loy Krathong celebrations have expanded beyond the traditional krathong floating. Fireworks light up the sky, lanterns known as "khom loi" are released into the air, and cultural performances take place on grand stages. Visitors can immerse themselves in the festivities, participating in traditional games, enjoying delectable street food, and witnessing awe-inspiring beauty pageants.

III. Top Destinations to Experience Loy Krathon:

Chiang Mai: As one of the cultural hubs of Thailand, Chiang Mai offers an unforgettable Loy Krathong experience. The ancient city walls become adorned with lights and lanterns, and the picturesque Mae Ping River sets the stage for the release of thousands of krathongs. The Yi Peng Lantern Festival, held concurrently with Loy Krathong, showcases the release of thousands of glowing lanterns into the night sky, creating a breathtaking spectacle.

Bangkok: The capital city of Thailand, Bangkok, celebrates Loy Krathong with great fervor. The Chao Phraya River becomes the focal point, with magnificent displays of floating krathongs and grand fireworks illuminating the night sky. The historic district of Rattanakosin Island hosts cultural performances, traditional food markets, and vibrant street processions, providing a captivating Loy Krathong experience.

Sukhothai: The birthplace of Loy Krathong, Sukhothai offers a unique and authentic celebration. The UNESCO World Heritage Site of Sukhothai Historical Park provides a stunning backdrop for the festival. Visitors can witness ancient rituals, enjoy traditional dance performances, and explore the beautifully illuminated ruins. The atmosphere in Sukhothai during Loy Krathong is truly enchanting, capturing the festival's historical essence.

Ayutthaya: Known for its rich historical heritage, Ayutthaya hosts a grand Loy Krathong event. The city's ancient temples, such as Wat Phra Si Sanphet and Wat Chaiwatthanaram, are adorned with lights, creating a mesmerizing ambiance. The riverbanks of the Chao Phraya River transform into vibrant marketplaces, offering delectable Thai cuisine and handmade crafts. The combination of ancient ruins and enchanting celebrations makes Ayutthaya a must-visit destination during Loy Krathong.

Phuket: The island paradise of Phuket celebrates Loy Krathong with its own unique twist. Patong Beach becomes the epicenter of festivities, with lively parades, beauty contests, and an impressive display of fireworks. Krathongs are floated on the sea, creating a breathtaking scene against the backdrop of the stunning coastline. Phuket offers a vibrant and modern Loy Krathong experience, infused with its own distinct charm.

The Loy Krathong Festival in Thailand offers a remarkable blend of cultural heritage, spirituality, and visual splendor. The captivating rituals, breathtaking displays of lights, and the joyous atmosphere create an enchanting experience for both locals and tourists. As a top tourist destination, Loy Krathong beckons visitors from around the world to immerse themselves in this awe-inspiring celebration. Whether you choose to participate in the festivities in Chiang Mai, Bangkok, Sukhothai, Ayutthaya, or Phuket, the magic of Loy Krathong will undoubtedly leave an indelible impression. So, prepare to release your krathong, make your wishes, and join the millions who gather to celebrate this extraordinary festival in the Land of Smiles.

•Songkran Festival

Thailand, known as the "Land of Smiles," is a country rich in cultural traditions and festivals. Among the numerous festivals celebrated in Thailand, Songkran stands out as one of the most vibrant and popular events. As the Thai

New Year festival, Songkran is a unique and exciting experience that attracts travelers from all around the world. In this Thailand travel guide, we will explore the significance of the Songkran Festival and why it has become a top tourist destination in the country.

Historical and Cultural Significance of Songkran Festival:

The Songkran Festival is deeply rooted in Thai culture and has historical and religious significance. The word "Songkran" comes from the Sanskrit language, meaning "astrological passage." The festival marks the traditional Thai New Year and celebrates the arrival of spring. It is also a time for Thais to pay respects to their ancestors and seek blessings for the upcoming year.

Date and Duration of the Festival:

Songkran Festival takes place annually from April 13th to 15th, although the duration can vary in different regions of Thailand. The festival originated as a single-day event, but over time it has expanded into a three-day water festival filled with joyous celebrations and cultural activities.

Water-Fighting Tradition:

The water-fighting aspect of the Songkran Festival is what makes it truly unique and exhilarating. During Songkran, locals and tourists alike take to the streets armed with water guns, buckets, and hoses, drenching each other in water. This symbolic act represents cleansing and washing away the misfortunes of the previous year, embracing the new beginning that comes with the Thai New Year.

Festivities and Cultural Activities:
Apart from the water fights, the Songkran Festival offers a range of cultural activities that give visitors a deeper insight into Thai traditions and customs. These activities include:

a) Traditional Ceremonies: Temples across the country hold ceremonies where locals make merit, offer food to monks, and perform rituals to honor their ancestors.

b) Buddha Processions: Elaborate processions featuring Buddha statues are carried through the streets, accompanied by colorful parades, music, and traditional dances.

c) Cultural Performances: Visitors can enjoy traditional Thai music, dance performances, and folk plays, showcasing the country's artistic heritage.

d) Street Markets: During Songkran, bustling street markets offer a plethora of traditional Thai street food, handicrafts, and souvenirs. Exploring these markets is a treat for food lovers and shopaholics.

Regional Variations:

While the Songkran Festival is celebrated throughout Thailand, different regions have their own unique customs and traditions. Some of the notable regional variations include:

a) Bangkok: In the capital city, Songkran is a lively affair, with the iconic Khao San Road becoming the epicenter of water fights and street parties.

b) Chiang Mai: Chiang Mai is renowned for having the most elaborate Songkran celebrations in Thailand. The city hosts the "Songkran Parade of the Goddess of Water," featuring intricately decorated floats and traditional performances.

c) Phuket: In Phuket, Songkran coincides with the "Patong Beach Festival," where locals and tourists gather for water fights and beachside activities.

Tips for Enjoying Songkran Festival:
To fully immerse yourself in the Songkran Festival experience, consider the following tips:

a) Dress Appropriately: Wear light and quick-drying clothes that you don't mind getting wet. It is also advisable to wear a waterproof bag to protect your valuables.

b) Protect Electronics: Seal your phones, cameras, and other electronics in waterproof pouches or plastic bags.

c) Respect Local Customs: While the festival is joyous and playful, remember to be respectful of the cultural significance and avoid water fights near temples or on sacred grounds.

d) Stay Hydrated: With the hot Thai weather, it is crucial to stay hydrated during the festivities. Carry a water bottle and drink plenty of fluids.

e) Stay Safe: Be cautious while participating in water fights and follow the instructions of local authorities to ensure a safe and enjoyable experience.

Songkran Festival Beyond Water Fights:
While the water fights are undoubtedly the highlight of the Songkran Festival, visitors can explore other attractions in Thailand during this time as well. Some recommendations include:

a) Visit Historical Sites: Explore the majestic temples, such as Wat Arun and Wat Phra Kaew in Bangkok, or the ancient ruins of Ayutthaya, to delve deeper into Thailand's rich history.

b) Nature and Adventure: Thailand boasts breathtaking natural landscapes. Explore national parks, go trekking in the jungles, or relax on the stunning beaches and islands.

c) Thai Cuisine: Indulge in the tantalizing flavors of Thai cuisine. From street food to fine dining, Thailand offers a culinary journey like no other.

d) Spa and Wellness: Treat yourself to traditional Thai massages and rejuvenating spa treatments, known for their therapeutic benefits.

The Songkran Festival is a truly unique and exhilarating experience that has made Thailand a top tourist destination. With its rich cultural significance, lively water fights, and a range of traditional activities, Songkran offers visitors an opportunity to immerse themselves in Thai traditions and celebrations. So, if you're planning a trip to Thailand, consider timing your visit during Songkran and join in the vibrant festivities that capture the essence of Thai culture and hospitality.

•Yi Peng Lantern Festival

Thailand, known for its rich cultural heritage and vibrant celebrations, is home to a myriad of festivals that showcase the country's unique traditions. One such captivating event is the Yi Peng Lantern Festival, a mesmerizing celebration that takes place annually in the northern region of Thailand. This travel guide delves into the essence of the Yi Peng Lantern Festival, providing an immersive experience of this remarkable event.

Origins and Significance of the Yi Peng Lantern Festival :

The origins of the Yi Peng Lantern Festival can be traced back to ancient Lanna Kingdom traditions, deeply rooted in Buddhist customs. Celebrated on the full moon of the twelfth lunar month, typically in November, this festival holds immense spiritual significance for Thai locals. The release of thousands of lanterns into the night sky symbolizes the act of letting go of negativity, making wishes, and bringing good luck.

Chiang Mai: The Epitome of Yi Peng :

Chiang Mai, the cultural capital of northern Thailand, serves as the epicenter of the Yi Peng Lantern Festival. Travelers from across the globe flock to this charming city to witness and participate in the festivities. The old city walls, adorned with intricate temples and historic landmarks, provide an enchanting backdrop to this captivating event.

2.1 Preparing for Yi Peng:
Before immersing oneself in the Yi Peng Lantern Festival, it is essential to understand the customs and preparations involved. Visitors can engage in workshops to learn the

art of making lanterns and receive guidance on proper etiquette during the festival. This hands-on experience offers a deeper connection to the festival's traditions.

2.2 Yi Peng Parade and Procession:
The festival kicks off with a vibrant parade through the streets of Chiang Mai. Elaborately decorated floats, traditional dancers, and mesmerizing music create a jubilant atmosphere. Locals and tourists alike gather to witness this procession, captivated by the colorful costumes and exuberant celebrations.

Lantern Release Ceremony :
The pinnacle of the Yi Peng Lantern Festival is the awe-inspiring lantern release ceremony. As night falls, thousands of paper lanterns, known as "khom loi," are lit and released into the sky simultaneously. The sight of countless glowing lanterns floating gracefully upwards is a truly magical experience, evoking a sense of tranquility and spiritual connection.
3.1 Mae Jo Lantern Release :
The grounds of Mae Jo University serve as the primary venue for the mass lantern release ceremony. Participants gather on the open fields, and at a designated time, the lanterns are simultaneously launched, creating a

breathtaking spectacle. The beauty of this synchronized release is truly unparalleled.

3.2 Private Lantern Releases :
For a more intimate experience, visitors can partake in private lantern releases organized by local temples and communities. These smaller-scale events offer a serene and personal ambiance, allowing individuals to reflect on their wishes and aspirations as their lantern ascends into the night sky. Engaging in a private lantern release provides a deeper connection to the festival's spiritual roots.

Exploring Chiang Mai Beyond Yi Peng :
While the Yi Peng Lantern Festival steals the spotlight, Chiang Mai has much more to offer for travelers. Take advantage of your visit to explore the city's other attractions, such as:
4.1 Temples and Wats :
Chiang Mai boasts a plethora of breathtaking temples and wats. Wat Phra That Doi Suthep, perched atop a mountain, offers panoramic views of the city, while Wat Chedi Luang, with its ancient ruins, exudes a sense of historical grandeur.

4.2 Night Bazaars and Local Cuisine :

Indulge in the vibrant night bazaars that come alive with a myriad of stalls selling traditional handicrafts, clothing, and delectable street food. Savor the local cuisine, from mouth-watering street-side delicacies to authentic Northern Thai dishes.

4.3 Elephant Sanctuaries and Nature:
Embark on an ethical elephant sanctuary visit, where you can interact with these majestic creatures in a responsible manner. Explore the lush landscapes surrounding Chiang Mai, which offer opportunities for trekking, zip-lining, and experiencing the region's natural beauty.

The Yi Peng Lantern Festival is an extraordinary cultural event that captures the hearts of visitors from around the world. Chiang Mai, with its enchanting atmosphere and rich heritage, serves as the perfect backdrop for this magical celebration. As you release your lantern into the night sky, immerse yourself in the spiritual significance of the festival, and take the opportunity to explore the wonders of Chiang Mai beyond Yi Peng. Prepare for an unforgettable journey through Thailand's cultural splendor, where tradition, spirituality, and natural beauty intertwine to create an experience like no other.

CHAPTER FIVE

Outdoor Activities and Adventure

• *Scuba Diving and Snorkeling*

Thailand, with its breathtaking landscapes, vibrant culture, and exotic cuisine, has long been a favorite destination for travelers seeking diverse experiences. Among its many treasures, Thailand is renowned for its remarkable underwater world, attracting scuba diving and snorkeling enthusiasts from around the globe. This travel guide will delve into the captivating realm of scuba diving and snorkeling in Thailand, providing invaluable insights into the best dive sites, marine life encounters, safety measures, and essential tips for an unforgettable adventure beneath the surface. Whether you're an experienced diver or a novice snorkeler, Thailand's azure waters offer an unparalleled opportunity to explore a diverse array of coral reefs, vibrant marine ecosystems, and encounter captivating marine species.

Thailand's Underwater Paradise

Thailand is blessed with a multitude of scuba diving and snorkeling spots that showcase the country's remarkable biodiversity. From the crystal-clear waters of the Andaman Sea to the glistening Gulf of Thailand, there are numerous destinations to discover. Some of the most renowned locations include the Similan Islands, Phi Phi Islands, Surin Islands, Koh Tao, and the vibrant reefs of the Koh Lanta Marine National Park. These destinations boast a kaleidoscope of marine life, including tropical fish, sea turtles, manta rays, whale sharks, and even the elusive leopard sharks. Explorers can also marvel at vibrant coral gardens, underwater caves, and submerged rock formations, providing a visually stunning and immersive experience.

Scuba Diving in Thailand

a. Dive Sites: Thailand offers a diverse range of dive sites catering to all experience levels. The Similan Islands, located in the Andaman Sea, are a paradise for advanced divers, featuring dramatic granite boulders, vibrant coral reefs, and encounters with majestic manta rays. The Phi Phi Islands offer an exciting mix of wall diving, stunning limestone formations, and the opportunity to witness blacktip reef sharks. Koh Tao, known as the "Turtle Island," is a haven for novice divers, with calm waters, shallow dive sites, and an abundance of sea turtles. The Richelieu Rock, located in the Surin Islands, is a must-visit for experienced divers, renowned for its remarkable biodiversity and the chance to spot whale sharks.

b. Diving Courses: Thailand is an excellent place to learn scuba diving, with numerous dive schools offering certification courses. Koh Tao, in particular, is renowned for its affordable and comprehensive dive training programs. Whether you're a complete beginner or looking to enhance your skills, qualified instructors will guide you through theory, pool training, and open water dives, ensuring a safe and enjoyable learning experience.

c. Safety and Conservation: While exploring the underwater world, safety should be a top priority. It is crucial to choose reputable dive operators that prioritize safety measures, provide well-maintained equipment, and adhere to international diving standards. Additionally, responsible diving practices, such as proper buoyancy control and respectful behavior towards marine life, are essential to minimize ecological impact and preserve the delicate ecosystems.

Snorkeling in Thailand

a. Snorkeling Spots: Snorkeling in Thailand offers a fantastic alternative to scuba diving, allowing travelers to witness the beauty of the underwater realm without extensive training. Popular snorkeling destinations include the idyllic Maya Bay in Phi Phi Islands, where vibrant coral reefs and tropical fish abound. The pristine beaches of Koh Lipe offer easy access to dazzling snorkeling sites, including Hin Ngam Bay and Koh Kra, known for their crystal-clear waters and diverse marine life. The vibrant Racha Islands, located near Phuket, boast colorful reefs teeming with anemones, clownfish, and other captivating species.

b. Equipment and Safety: Snorkeling requires minimal equipment, making it an accessible activity for all ages and skill levels. Snorkelers should invest in quality masks, snorkels, and fins to ensure comfort and ease while exploring the underwater wonders. Beginners should practice proper snorkeling techniques, such as clearing the snorkel and swimming with fins, to enhance safety and enjoyment. It is also essential to be aware of current and tidal conditions and avoid touching or disturbing marine life to preserve the fragile ecosystems.

Practical Tips and Cultural Considerations

a. Best Time to Visit: Thailand's diving and snorkeling season varies between the Andaman Sea (west coast) and the Gulf of Thailand (east coast). The prime months for the Andaman Sea are November to April, offering calm waters, excellent visibility, and ideal conditions for diving and snorkeling. On the Gulf of Thailand side, the best time to visit is from May to September when the sea is calm, and underwater visibility is at its peak.

b. Planning and Booking: It is advisable to book diving or snorkeling trips in advance, especially during peak seasons, to secure your preferred dates and dive operators. Researching reputable operators, reading reviews, and comparing prices will help ensure a safe and enjoyable experience.

c. Cultural Sensitivity: Thailand has a rich cultural heritage, and visitors should respect local customs and traditions. When visiting dive and snorkel sites, it is essential to follow guidelines provided by dive operators, such as not touching or collecting marine life, and avoiding actions that could harm the delicate coral reefs.

Thailand's underwater world beckons adventurers with its awe-inspiring beauty and rich marine biodiversity. From the adrenaline rush of scuba diving to the tranquility of snorkeling, Thailand offers an array of experiences for all underwater enthusiasts. This travel guide has unveiled the treasures that lie beneath Thailand's azure waters, from the stunning dive sites and marine encounters to essential safety measures and cultural considerations. By embracing responsible diving practices and immersing oneself in the enchanting realm of Thailand's oceans, travelers can create unforgettable memories and contribute to the preservation of these remarkable underwater ecosystems. So, pack your gear, dive in, and prepare to be amazed by Thailand's aquatic wonders.

•Trekking and Jungle Tours

Thailand, known for its stunning landscapes and rich biodiversity, offers adventurous travelers a plethora of opportunities to explore its natural wonders through trekking and jungle tours. From dense rainforests and majestic mountains to hidden waterfalls and exotic wildlife, the country boasts a diverse range of ecosystems waiting to be discovered. This guide aims to provide an extensive overview of trekking and jungle tours in Thailand, including popular destinations, types of tours, essential tips, and a glimpse into the unique experiences awaiting intrepid explorers.

I. Popular Trekking and Jungle Tour Destinations:

Chiang Mai: Nestled in the lush hills of northern Thailand, Chiang Mai serves as a gateway to numerous trekking adventures. Explore the Doi Inthanon National Park, encounter hill tribes, and witness breathtaking vistas from the region's highest peak.

Khao Sok National Park: Located in southern Thailand, Khao Sok is a true jungle paradise. Embark on multi-day treks, discover the iconic limestone cliffs, and stay in floating bungalows on the stunning Cheow Lan Lake.

Pai: A charming town in the Mae Hong Son Province, Pai offers a laid-back atmosphere and a variety of trekking options. Trek through picturesque valleys, visit hot springs, and interact with the local Lisu and Karen hill tribes.

Krabi: Renowned for its stunning coastline, Krabi also boasts dense jungles and towering cliffs. Experience rock climbing, jungle hikes, and explore the Emerald Pool and Hot Springs in the nearby Khao Phra Bang Khram Nature Reserve

.

II. Types of Trekking and Jungle Tours:

Day Treks: Ideal for those with limited time, day treks provide a taste of Thailand's natural beauty. Embark on guided hikes to waterfalls, viewpoints, and through lush forests, often combined with visits to local communities.

Overnight Treks: For a more immersive experience, opt for overnight treks that involve camping in the wilderness. Sleep under the stars, indulge in local cuisine, and witness stunning sunrises or sunsets from mountaintops.

Multi-Day Jungle Tours: These tours range from two to several days and allow travelers to explore remote areas and encounter diverse wildlife. They often include activities like kayaking, bamboo rafting, and cave exploration.

Elephant Trekking: While controversial due to animal welfare concerns, some operators offer ethical elephant experiences where trekkers can observe and interact with elephants in their natural habitat.

III. Essential Tips for Trekking and Jungle Tours:

Choose a Reputable Tour Operator: Ensure your tour operator is licensed, has positive reviews, and adheres to sustainable and ethical practices.

Pack Wisely: Wear comfortable, lightweight clothing, and sturdy footwear suitable for trekking. Pack essentials like insect repellent, sunscreen, a hat, a raincoat, a first aid kit, and a refillable water bottle.

Stay Hydrated and Energized: Drink plenty of water to stay hydrated in the tropical climate, and carry energy-boosting snacks like nuts, energy bars, and fruits.
Respect Nature and Local Culture: Follow the principles of Leave No Trace, respect wildlife, and adhere to any cultural norms when visiting local communities or temples.

Prepare for Weather Conditions: Thailand's climate can be unpredictable, so be prepared for sudden rain showers or temperature changes. Carry appropriate gear and check the weather forecast before embarking on your trek.

IV. Unique Experiences in Trekking and Jungle Tours:

Hill Tribe Encounters: Immerse yourself in the rich cultural heritage of Thailand by visiting hill tribe communities like the Karen, Hmong, or Lisu. Learn about their traditions, sample local cuisine, and purchase handicrafts directly from the artisans.

Wildlife Spotting: Thailand's jungles are home to a diverse array of wildlife, including elephants, monkeys, tropical birds, and reptiles. Keep your eyes peeled during treks for a chance to observe these magnificent creatures in their natural habitat.

Overnight Camping: Spend a night under the starry sky, enjoying the tranquility of nature. Listen to the sounds of the forest, share stories around a campfire, and wake up to the harmonious chorus of birds.

Waterfall Exploration: Discover hidden cascades nestled within the lush jungle. Take refreshing dips, capture memorable photographs, and let the soothing sounds of the water rejuvenate your senses.

Trekking and jungle tours in Thailand offer an incredible opportunity to connect with nature, explore diverse ecosystems, and immerse oneself in the vibrant local culture. Whether it's venturing through dense forests, meeting indigenous communities, or encountering exotic wildlife, Thailand's natural beauty provides a memorable and rewarding adventure for travelers seeking an off-the-beaten-path experience. By choosing responsible operators and embracing sustainable practices, visitors can contribute to the preservation of Thailand's precious natural heritage for generations to come. So, lace up your boots, pack your sense of adventure, and embark on a trekking or jungle tour that will leave you with lifelong memories of this enchanting Southeast Asian gem.

•Rock Climbing in Railay

Thailand is renowned for its breathtaking landscapes, idyllic beaches, and vibrant culture. Amidst the numerous travel destinations in this Southeast Asian gem, Railay stands out as a must-visit location for adventure enthusiasts. Nestled on the Andaman Sea, Railay is a small peninsula accessible only by boat, offering a secluded haven for rock climbers from around the world. Boasting towering limestone cliffs, crystal-clear waters, and a vibrant climbing community, Railay has earned a reputation as one of Asia's premier rock climbing destinations. This comprehensive travel guide will delve into the captivating world of rock climbing in Railay, providing all the essential information and tips to make the most of your climbing adventure in this Thai paradise.

I. Getting to Railay :

Railay is located on the southern coast of Thailand, near Krabi province. The nearest major airport is Krabi International Airport, which is well-connected to various domestic and international destinations. From the airport, travelers can easily reach Railay by taking a taxi or shared minivan to Ao Nang, followed by a short boat ride to Railay. Alternatively, if you're coming from Phuket, you can take a ferry directly to Railay, offering a scenic journey across the Andaman Sea.

II. Overview of Rock Climbing in Railay :

Railay's towering limestone cliffs have drawn climbers from all corners of the globe, making it a world-class rock climbing destination. The peninsula offers a diverse range of climbing routes suitable for climbers of all levels, from beginners to seasoned professionals. The climbing styles in Railay include sport climbing, traditional climbing, and deep water soloing (DWS). The area's unique karst formations provide an abundance of pockets, crimps, and tufas, offering an exciting challenge for climbers.

III. Climbing Zones and Routes :

a) East Railay: The eastern side of Railay offers a multitude of climbing routes, predominantly in the intermediate to advanced range. Popular areas include Phra Nang Cave, Diamond Cave, and Thaiwand Wall. Phra Nang Cave is known for its iconic stalactite features and hosts several classic routes such as "Humanality" and "The Ladder."

b) Tonsai: Located on the western side of Railay, Tonsai is a vibrant climbing community with a laid-back atmosphere. Tonsai is famous for its overhanging routes and challenging climbing grades. Notable climbing spots in Tonsai include The Keep, Dum's Kitchen, and Eagle Wall.

c) Railay West: Railay West offers a mix of climbing routes suitable for beginners and intermediate climbers. The picturesque beachside cliffs provide a stunning backdrop for climbing adventures. Popular routes in this area include "123 Wall" and "Groove Tube."

d) Deep Water Soloing (DWS): Railay is also renowned for its DWS opportunities, where climbers scale the cliffs without the use of ropes or harnesses and plunge into the deep waters below. Tonsai Bay and Phra Nang Cave are popular spots for DWS, offering an exhilarating and refreshing experience.

IV. Climbing Seasons and Weather :
The ideal time to visit Railay for rock climbing is during the dry season, which extends from November to April. During this period, the weather is generally stable with lower humidity levels, providing excellent climbing conditions. The peak season falls between December and February when the temperatures are slightly cooler. However, Railay can get crowded during this time, so planning in advance and booking accommodations and climbing courses ahead of time is advisable. The monsoon season, from May to October, brings heavy rainfall and rough sea conditions, making climbing unsafe and less enjoyable.

V. Climbing Courses and Guided Tours :
For beginners or those looking to enhance their climbing skills, Railay offers a variety of climbing courses and guided tours. Local climbing schools and experienced instructors

provide comprehensive instruction on techniques, safety, and equipment. These courses cater to climbers of all levels, from introductory sessions to advanced skills training. Whether you're a complete novice or seeking to tackle challenging routes, these courses ensure a safe and rewarding climbing experience.

VI. Essential Tips and Safety Guidelines:

a) Equipment: While it's possible to rent climbing gear in Railay, bringing your own equipment is recommended, especially if you have specific preferences or requirements. Ensure your gear is in good condition and suitable for the limestone rock type.

b) Climbing Grades: Familiarize yourself with the climbing grading system used in Railay, as it may differ from other regions. The routes are typically graded using the French numerical system, ranging from 5a (easiest) to 9c (most challenging).

c) Safety Measures: Prioritize safety at all times and adhere to established safety protocols. Double-check knots, harnesses, and belay systems. Climbing with a partner and using proper communication techniques is essential.

d) Hydration and Sun Protection: Railay's tropical climate can be intense, so staying hydrated and protecting yourself from the sun's rays are crucial. Carry plenty of water, wear sunscreen, and consider climbing during the cooler parts of the day.

VII. Accommodations and Amenities :

Railay offers a range of accommodations catering to different budgets and preferences. From basic bungalows to luxurious beachfront resorts, there is something for everyone. Accommodations are clustered around Railay East and West, providing easy access to the climbing areas. Railay also has various restaurants, bars, and shops where climbers can relax and socialize after a day of climbing.

Railay's stunning limestone cliffs, azure waters, and welcoming climbing community make it a paradise for rock climbing enthusiasts. The diverse range of climbing routes, the availability of climbing courses, and the breathtaking natural surroundings make Railay an unforgettable destination for climbers of all levels. Whether you're a novice seeking an introduction to the sport or an experienced climber looking for new challenges, Railay has something to offer. So pack your gear, prepare for an adrenaline-filled adventure, and get ready to conquer the cliffs of Railay in Thailand's ultimate climbing paradise.

•Elephant Sanctuaries and Wildlife Reserves

Thailand, renowned for its rich cultural heritage, stunning landscapes, and diverse wildlife, offers an incredible opportunity to experience the wonders of nature. Among its most cherished attractions are the elephant sanctuaries and wildlife reserves that provide a safe haven for these majestic creatures. In this comprehensive travel guide, we will delve into the enchanting world of elephant sanctuaries and wildlife reserves in Thailand, highlighting their significance, conservation efforts, and the unforgettable experiences they offer to visitors.

I. Understanding Elephant Sanctuaries:

Historical Significance:

Elephants in Thai Culture: Elephants hold a special place in Thai culture, symbolizing strength, wisdom, and prosperity.
Logging Industry Impact: The decline of the logging industry in the 20th century led to the need for alternative means of supporting elephants and their mahouts (caretakers).
Purpose and Conservation Efforts:

Transition to Sanctuaries: Elephant sanctuaries emerged as a humane alternative to elephant rides and performances, focusing on rehabilitation, education, and ethical tourism.
Rescue and Rehabilitation: Sanctuaries rescue elephants from exploitative practices and provide them with a safe environment to heal physically and emotionally.
Community Involvement: Sanctuaries collaborate with local communities to create sustainable models that benefit both elephants and humans.
Ethical Tourism Practices:

No Riding Policy: Many sanctuaries prioritize the well-being of elephants, prohibiting riding to prevent injury and stress.

Observing Natural Behaviors: Visitors can observe elephants in their natural habitat, witnessing their social interactions, bathing rituals, and feeding habits.

Volunteer Programs: Some sanctuaries offer volunteer programs where visitors can actively contribute to the elephants' care and conservation.

II. Exploring Elephant Sanctuaries:

Popular Elephant Sanctuaries:

Elephant Nature Park (Chiang Mai): Known for its rescue efforts and extensive elephant care programs.

Boon Lott's Elephant Sanctuary (Sukhothai): Focuses on the well-being and happiness of elephants, providing them with vast natural landscapes.

Wildlife Friends Foundation Thailand (Petchaburi): Rescues not only elephants but also other wildlife species, promoting conservation and education.

Unique Experiences:

Bathing and Feeding Elephants: Interact with elephants in their natural habitat by bathing them in rivers or feeding them their favorite treats.

Mahout Training: Gain insights into the daily lives of mahouts, learning about their bond with elephants and their traditional knowledge.

Educational Programs: Participate in educational activities and workshops to understand the challenges elephants face and the importance of conservation.

III. Exploring Wildlife Reserves:

National Parks and Reserves:

Khao Yai National Park: One of Thailand's oldest and most famous national parks, known for its diverse wildlife, including elephants, tigers, and gibbons.

Kaeng Krachan National Park: A vast and scenic park offering a chance to spot rare bird species, deer, and elephants in their natural habitat.

Huai Kha Khaeng Wildlife Sanctuary: A UNESCO World Heritage Site, known for its significant population of tigers, leopards, and elephants.

Wildlife Conservation and Activities:

Guided Safaris: Explore the reserves on guided safaris, led by experienced rangers who share insights into the park's ecosystem and wildlife.

Bird Watching: Thailand is a birdwatcher's paradise, with numerous species of resident and migratory birds to be found in its wildlife reserves.

Nature Trails and Trekking: Discover the natural beauty of the reserves by embarking on nature trails and trekking adventures, offering opportunities to observe wildlife up close.

IV. Responsible Tourism and Conservation:

Choosing Ethical Sanctuaries and Reserves:

Research and Prioritize Animal Welfare: Select sanctuaries and reserves that prioritize the well-being and ethical treatment of animals.

Avoid Exploitative Practices: Refrain from supporting attractions that involve elephant riding, performing tricks, or any form of wildlife exploitation.

Supporting Local Communities:

Community-Based Tourism: Engage in community-based tourism initiatives that involve local communities and promote their sustainable development.

Support Conservation Efforts: Contribute to conservation initiatives through donations or by participating in volunteer programs.

Thailand's elephant sanctuaries and wildlife reserves provide visitors with a unique and ethical opportunity to experience the country's magnificent wildlife up close. Through their conservation efforts and focus on responsible tourism, these sanctuaries and reserves play a crucial role in protecting endangered species and promoting the well-being of elephants. By choosing ethical practices and supporting local communities, travelers can make a positive impact while creating unforgettable memories in the captivating natural landscapes of Thailand.

CHAPTER SIX

Thai Islands and Beaches

•*Koh Samui*

Koh Samui, an island located in the Gulf of Thailand, has emerged as one of the top travel destinations in Southeast Asia. With its palm-fringed beaches, crystal-clear waters, lush rainforests, and vibrant culture, Koh Samui offers a truly enchanting experience for travelers. In this comprehensive Thailand travel guide, we will delve into the beauty and attractions of Koh Samui, helping you plan your perfect tropical getaway.

History and Culture

Koh Samui has a rich history that dates back over 1,500 years. Originally a fishing community, the island's culture has been influenced by Chinese, Malay, and Southern Thai traditions. Buddhism plays a significant role in the lives of the locals, and visitors can witness ornate Buddhist temples, such as Wat Plai Laem and Wat Khunaram. The famous Big

Buddha, a 12-meter-tall golden statue, is a prominent landmark on the island.

Beaches and Water Activities

Koh Samui boasts stunning beaches that cater to different tastes. Chaweng Beach, the most popular and developed, offers a vibrant nightlife scene and a wide range of water sports activities, including jet skiing, snorkeling, and diving. For a more tranquil experience, head to Lamai Beach, known for its relaxed atmosphere and picturesque surroundings. Bophut Beach, with its charming Fisherman's Village, combines a serene beach setting with traditional Thai architecture and trendy restaurants.

Natural Wonders and Outdoor Adventures

Beyond its beaches, Koh Samui is blessed with natural wonders. Ang Thong National Marine Park, an archipelago of 42 islands, is a must-visit for nature enthusiasts. Explore the emerald lagoons, pristine beaches, and lush jungles through kayaking, hiking, and snorkeling. Hin Ta and Hin Yai, also known as the Grandfather and Grandmother Rocks, are intriguing rock formations that have become a popular tourist attraction.

Temples and Spiritual Retreats

Koh Samui offers a serene atmosphere for spiritual retreats and introspection. Wat Samret is a peaceful temple nestled in the mountains, offering breathtaking panoramic views of the island. For a more immersive experience, retreat centers like Kamalaya and The Yogarden provide yoga and meditation classes, detox programs, and holistic healing treatments. These sanctuaries allow visitors to rejuvenate their mind, body, and soul.

Nightlife and Entertainment

Koh Samui comes alive after sunset with its vibrant nightlife scene. Chaweng Beach Road and Lamai Beach are dotted with bars, clubs, and live music venues where visitors can dance the night away. The famous Ark Bar Beach Resort hosts popular beach parties with fire shows and international DJs. For a more laid-back evening, Fisherman's Village offers a charming atmosphere with its seaside restaurants and local street performers.

Culinary Delights

Koh Samui is a food lover's paradise, offering a diverse range of culinary delights. Indulge in traditional Thai cuisine, with dishes like pad

Thai, green curry, and tom yum goong. The island also boasts a plethora of seafood options, with fresh catches served at beachside restaurants. Don't miss the opportunity to try street food at night markets, where you can sample local favorites like mango sticky rice and grilled satay skewers.

Koh Samui, with its stunning beaches, natural wonders, rich culture, and vibrant nightlife, is a tropical paradise that captures the hearts of travelers from around the world. Whether you seek relaxation, adventure, or spiritual rejuvenation, this Thai island offers an unforgettable experience. As you plan your trip, consider the various attractions and activities Koh Samui has to offer, ensuring a well-rounded exploration of this idyllic destination. Embark on a journey to Koh Samui, and immerse yourself in the beauty and warmth of Thailand's jewel in the Gulf of Thailand.

•Koh Tao

Koh Tao, a mesmerizing island located in the Gulf of Thailand, is a true gem awaiting discovery. Known as the "Turtle Island," this small paradise offers breathtaking landscapes, vibrant coral reefs, and a laid-back atmosphere that attracts travelers from around the world. In this comprehensive Thailand travel guide, we will explore the wonders of Koh Tao, including its stunning beaches, vibrant marine life, thrilling water sports, diverse cuisine, and top attractions. Get ready to immerse yourself in the beauty and tranquility of Koh Tao.

Getting to Koh Tao:

To reach Koh Tao, you have two main options. Firstly, you can take a flight from Bangkok to Samui International Airport and then catch a ferry to the island, which takes around 2-3 hours. Alternatively, you can take an overnight train or bus from Bangkok to Chumphon and then hop on a ferry to Koh Tao, with the journey lasting approximately 8-10 hours. Whichever route you choose, the journey itself offers glimpses of Thailand's picturesque landscapes.

Beaches and Bays:

Koh Tao boasts numerous stunning beaches, each with its unique charm. Sairee Beach is the most popular and vibrant, with a long stretch of white sand, crystal-clear waters, and a bustling beachfront lined with restaurants, bars, and shops. Other noteworthy beaches include Freedom Beach, Shark Bay, and Tanote Bay, where you can relax, sunbathe, and soak up the tropical vibes. Snorkeling and diving enthusiasts will find paradise at Mango Bay and Aow Leuk, renowned for their abundant marine life and colorful coral reefs.

Diving and Snorkeling:
Koh Tao is a world-renowned diving destination, attracting both beginners and experienced divers. The island offers numerous dive centers and schools where you can obtain your diving certification or embark on thrilling diving expeditions. Explore the vibrant coral gardens, encounter exotic marine species, and discover stunning underwater landscapes at popular dive sites such as Chumphon Pinnacle, Sail Rock, and Shark Island. For snorkelers, shallow coral reefs near the shores provide opportunities to witness the beauty of tropical fish and other marine creatures.

Water Sports and Outdoor Activities:

Beyond diving and snorkeling, Koh Tao offers a plethora of water sports and outdoor activities to suit all tastes. Kayaking along the island's coastline allows you to discover hidden coves and secluded beaches. Stand-up paddleboarding is another fantastic option to explore the calm turquoise waters. Adventure seekers can try cliff jumping at Sai Nuan Beach or engage in exhilarating activities such as jet skiing, wakeboarding, and sailing. Hiking enthusiasts can trek to the island's viewpoints, such as John-Suwan Viewpoint, to marvel at panoramic vistas of the island and its surrounding beauty.

Island Hopping:

Koh Tao serves as a perfect base for exploring the nearby islands. Take a day trip to Koh Nang Yuan, a trio of small islands connected by sandbars, offering postcard-perfect views and excellent snorkeling opportunities. Koh Nang Yuan is just a short boat ride away and is often considered one of the most beautiful islands in the region. Additionally, you can visit Koh Samui and Koh Phangan, known for their pristine beaches, lively nightlife, and cultural attractions.

Dining and Nightlife:

Koh Tao presents an array of dining options that cater to all tastes and budgets. From traditional Thai cuisine to international dishes, beachside shacks to upscale restaurants, you'll find it all here. Indulge in freshly caught seafood, savor traditional curries and pad Thai, and relish the tantalizing flavors of Thai street food. As the sun sets, the island comes alive with beach parties, fire shows, and live music. The lively bars and clubs on Sairee Beach offer a vibrant nightlife scene where you can dance the night away or simply unwind with a cocktail in hand.

Land Attractions:
While the underwater world steals the spotlight on Koh Tao, the island also offers captivating land-based attractions. Visit the Wat Koh Tao, a charming Buddhist temple perched on a hilltop, providing stunning panoramic views. The Koh Tao Viewpoint is another must-visit spot, offering breathtaking vistas of the island and its surrounding waters. For a touch of adventure, explore the island's rocky cliffs, hidden bays, and lush jungles on an ATV or motorbike tour.

Koh Tao, with its breathtaking beaches, world-class diving spots, vibrant marine life, and laid-back island vibe, offers an unforgettable tropical getaway. Whether you seek relaxation, adventure, or a mix of both, this Thailand travel guide has unveiled the wonders of Koh Tao. Immerse yourself in the turquoise waters, explore the colorful coral reefs, indulge in delicious cuisine, and create memories that will last a lifetime in this tropical paradise. Embark on your journey to Koh Tao and let its beauty captivate your soul.

•Koh Chang

Koh Chang, also known as the "Elephant Island," is a hidden gem nestled in the Gulf of Thailand. Renowned for its untouched natural beauty, pristine beaches, lush rainforests, and diverse marine life, Koh Chang offers a unique travel experience for those seeking tranquility and adventure. In this comprehensive Thailand travel guide, we will explore the captivating allure of Koh Chang, including its attractions, activities, accommodations, cuisine, and practical tips for a memorable journey.

Geographical and Historical Overview:

Located in Trat Province, about 315 kilometers southeast of Bangkok, Koh Chang is the second largest island in Thailand. With an area of approximately 429 square kilometers, it is part of the Mu Ko Chang National Park, renowned for its rich biodiversity and protected marine ecosystems. The island's history dates back to the late Ayutthaya period, and it has witnessed the rise and fall of various kingdoms, including the French occupation during the 19th century.

Getting to Koh Chang:

Travelers can reach Koh Chang via different modes of transportation. The most convenient option is to take a flight to Trat Airport from Bangkok, followed by a short ferry ride to the island. Alternatively, there are buses and minivans available from Bangkok to the mainland pier, where ferries operate regularly to transport visitors to Koh Chang. Private transfers and organized tours are also available for a hassle-free journey.

Beaches and Natural Wonders:

Koh Chang boasts a collection of pristine beaches that cater to different preferences. White Sand Beach, the most popular stretch, offers a vibrant atmosphere with a variety of accommodations, restaurants, and nightlife options. For those seeking a quieter ambiance, Kai Bae Beach and Lonely Beach are ideal choices. Other remarkable beaches include Klong Prao Beach, Bang Bao Beach, and Long Beach, each showcasing unique charms and picturesque scenery.

Beyond the beaches, Koh Chang's dense rainforests beckon adventurers. Explore the island's interior on jungle treks, where experienced guides lead you through lush trails, hidden waterfalls, and diverse wildlife. Popular spots include the Klong Plu Waterfall, Than Mayom Waterfall, and Salakphet Mangrove Walkway, offering an opportunity to immerse in nature's serenity.

Marine Adventures:
Koh Chang is a haven for marine enthusiasts and offers a range of water activities. Snorkeling and scuba diving allow visitors to discover vibrant coral reefs teeming with colorful marine life. The nearby islands of Koh Rang, Koh Kra, and Koh Wai are renowned

diving hotspots, providing an unforgettable underwater experience. Kayaking, paddleboarding, and fishing are also popular options, allowing travelers to explore the crystal-clear waters and hidden coves at their own pace.

Island Excursions:

Embark on island-hopping adventures to explore Koh Chang's neighboring isles. Take a boat trip to Koh Mak, an idyllic island known for its tranquil atmosphere and pristine beaches. Discover Koh Kood, the fourth largest island in Thailand, boasting untouched nature, waterfalls, and charming fishing villages. These excursions offer a glimpse into the unspoiled beauty of the region and provide an escape from the crowds.

Cultural and Historical Sites:

Immerse yourself in Koh Chang's cultural heritage by visiting the historical sites scattered across the island. The Koh Chang Naval Battle Memorial serves as a reminder of the island's strategic significance during the Franco-Thai War. Wat Salak Phet, a Buddhist temple, offers a peaceful ambiance and panoramic views of the surrounding area. Exploring the local fishing villages, such as Bang Bao, grants insight into the islanders' traditional way of life.

Dining and Local Cuisine:

Koh Chang showcases a vibrant culinary scene, with numerous beachside restaurants and local eateries. Indulge in fresh seafood, including succulent grilled prawns, steamed fish, and delectable crab dishes. Don't miss out on the traditional Thai curries, pad Thai, and som tam (spicy papaya salad). Koh Chang also caters to international tastes, with various restaurants serving Western, Indian, and Mediterranean cuisines.

Accommodations and Resorts:

Koh Chang offers a wide range of accommodations, catering to all budgets and preferences. From luxurious beachfront resorts with private pools and spa facilities to boutique hotels, guesthouses, and budget-friendly bungalows, there is something for every traveler. Areas like White Sand Beach, Kai Bae, and Lonely Beach offer a variety of accommodation options, ensuring a comfortable stay.

Best Time to Visit and Practical Tips:

The best time to visit Koh Chang is during the dry season, which spans from November to April. The weather is pleasant, with clear skies and comfortable temperatures. Avoid the monsoon season, which typically occurs between May and October, as heavy rainfall and rough seas may limit outdoor activities. Remember to pack lightweight clothing, swimwear, sunscreen, insect repellent, and comfortable shoes for outdoor adventures.

Responsible Tourism and Conservation:
As a protected national park, Koh Chang places a strong emphasis on sustainable tourism. Travelers are encouraged to respect the island's natural beauty, refrain from littering, and follow responsible snorkeling and diving practices. Additionally, supporting local businesses, such as eco-friendly accommodations and community-based initiatives, contributes to the preservation of the island's fragile ecosystem and supports the local economy.

Koh Chang, with its pristine beaches, lush rainforests, and abundant marine life, offers an unparalleled travel experience in Thailand. Whether you seek relaxation on sandy shores, thrilling water adventures, or a deeper connection with nature, this island paradise has it all. By exploring the island's natural wonders, embracing its rich culture, and practicing responsible tourism, you will create cherished memories that will last a lifetime on Koh Chang.

•*Koh Lanta*

Nestled in the Andaman Sea off the southwestern coast of Thailand, Koh Lanta is a pristine island destination that promises a perfect blend of untouched natural beauty, warm Thai hospitality, and a laid-back atmosphere. This comprehensive travel guide will introduce you to the captivating island of Koh Lanta, providing valuable insights into its stunning beaches, diverse marine life, cultural experiences, adventurous activities, and much more. Get ready to embark on a journey to this tranquil paradise and discover why it should be on every traveler's bucket list.

Geography and Location:
Koh Lanta is part of the Krabi Province and is made up of several islands, the two main ones

being Koh Lanta Yai and Koh Lanta Noi. Koh Lanta Yai is the larger and more developed of the two, drawing the majority of tourists. With its strategic location, Koh Lanta serves as a gateway to numerous attractions in the region, including the famous Phi Phi Islands, Phang Nga Bay, and the stunning Railay Beach.

Getting to Koh Lanta:
Traveling to Koh Lanta is relatively easy, with various options available. The nearest international airport is Krabi International Airport, which is well-connected to major cities in Southeast Asia. From the airport, you can take a taxi or a shuttle bus to the Klong Jilad Pier, where regular ferries depart for Koh Lanta. Another option is to take a direct ferry from Phuket or Ao Nang.

Beaches of Koh Lanta:
Koh Lanta boasts an impressive coastline adorned with pristine sandy beaches and crystal-clear waters. Some of the must-visit beaches include:

a. Long Beach (Phra Ae Beach): Known for its powdery white sand, Long Beach offers a relaxed atmosphere and breathtaking sunsets. The beach is lined with beachfront resorts, restaurants, and bars, providing a perfect blend of tranquility and convenience.

b. Kantiang Bay: Tucked away in a secluded corner of the island, Kantiang Bay is a true tropical paradise. With its serene ambiance and dramatic cliffs, this beach is ideal for those seeking a peaceful escape.

c. Bamboo Bay: Offering a more secluded and off-the-beaten-path experience, Bamboo Bay is a hidden gem that showcases the unspoiled beauty of Koh Lanta. Its calm waters are perfect for swimming and snorkeling.

Marine Life and Diving:
Koh Lanta is renowned for its vibrant underwater world, making it a paradise for divers and snorkelers. The island offers a range of dive sites suitable for all levels of experience. Hin Daeng and Hin Muang are famous for their deep-sea diving experiences and the opportunity to spot majestic manta rays. Additionally, the nearby Koh Haa islands are known for their crystal-clear waters, colorful coral reefs, and diverse marine life.

Island Hopping:

Beyond the shores of Koh Lanta, an array of stunning islands awaits exploration. Koh Rok is a popular choice for day trips, offering pristine beaches, excellent snorkeling, and a vibrant marine ecosystem. The four islands of Koh Mook, Koh Kradan, Koh Ngai, and Koh Libong also beckon with their natural beauty and tranquility.

Local Culture and Cuisine:
Exploring the local culture is an integral part of any trip to Thailand, and Koh Lanta offers a glimpse into the traditional way of life. Visit Old Town, situated on Koh Lanta's east coast, to discover its charming wooden houses, Chinese-style shop fronts, and vibrant local markets. Don't miss the chance to savor authentic Thai cuisine, including mouthwatering seafood delicacies, spicy curries, and delicious street food offerings.

Adventure Activities:
Koh Lanta presents an array of thrilling activities for adventure enthusiasts. Embark on a kayaking excursion through the island's mangrove forests, and marvel at the unique ecosystem teeming with wildlife. Take a jungle trek to explore lush rainforests, hidden waterfalls, and panoramic viewpoints. For

adrenaline junkies, rock climbing and cliff jumping are popular options, with numerous climbing routes available for different skill levels.

Sustainable Tourism and Conservation Efforts:
Koh Lanta takes pride in its commitment to sustainable tourism and conservation. The island actively promotes eco-friendly practices, with several resorts and organizations dedicated to protecting the marine environment and preserving the island's natural resources. Travelers are encouraged to support responsible tourism initiatives and minimize their impact on the fragile ecosystems.

Koh Lanta offers an idyllic escape from the bustling cities and tourist crowds, providing a perfect blend of natural beauty, adventure, cultural experiences, and relaxation. Whether you seek pristine beaches, thrilling underwater adventures, cultural exploration, or simply a peaceful retreat, Koh Lanta has something to offer every type of traveler. Embrace the island's charm, immerse yourself in its warm hospitality, and create memories that will last a lifetime in this serene Thai paradise.

CHAPTER SEVEN

Historical and Cultural Sites

• *Ayutthaya Historical Park*

Nestled in the heart of Thailand, Ayutthaya Historical Park stands as a testament to the rich cultural heritage and historical significance of the country. Located just a short distance north of Bangkok, Ayutthaya served as the capital of the Kingdom of Siam for over 400 years, from the 14th to the 18th century. Today, it is recognized as a UNESCO World Heritage site and is a popular destination for travelers seeking to delve into Thailand's glorious past. In this comprehensive Thailand travel guide, we will embark on a journey through time and discover the wonders that await within the Ayutthaya Historical Park.

History and Background:

1.1 The Rise of Ayutthaya:
Ayutthaya was founded in 1350 by King Ramathibodi I, who established it as the capital of the Ayutthaya Kingdom. The city quickly flourished into a bustling metropolis, becoming a major center of trade and a melting pot of diverse cultures. Ayutthaya's strategic location along the Chao Phraya River made it an essential hub for commerce and diplomacy, attracting merchants from Europe, China, India, and neighboring Southeast Asian countries.

1.2 The Golden Age:
During the 16th and 17th centuries, Ayutthaya reached its zenith as one of the wealthiest and most powerful cities in Asia. The kingdom experienced a golden age of art, architecture, and international trade. Temples, palaces, and monuments were erected, showcasing the splendor and opulence of the Ayutthaya civilization.

Exploring Ayutthaya Historical Park:

2.1 UNESCO World Heritage Site:
In 1991, Ayutthaya was designated as a UNESCO World Heritage site due to its outstanding universal value as an

archaeological site. The Ayutthaya Historical Park covers an extensive area of 289 hectares, encompassing the remains of the ancient city and its significant structures.

2.2 Temples and Ruins:
The park is home to numerous temples and ruins, each with its unique charm and historical significance. Wat Mahathat, with its iconic Buddha head entwined in the roots of a banyan tree, is one of the most famous and photographed sites in Ayutthaya. Wat Phra Si Sanphet, once a grand royal temple, features impressive restored chedis (stupas) that offer panoramic views of the park. Other notable temples include Wat Lokayasutharam, known for its enormous reclining Buddha statue, and Wat Chaiwatthanaram, an architectural masterpiece situated on the banks of the river.

Must-Visit Attractions in Ayutthaya:

3.1 Ayutthaya Historical Study Center:
For a deeper understanding of Ayutthaya's history, a visit to the Ayutthaya Historical Study Center is highly recommended. The center houses a wealth of artifacts, exhibits, and multimedia presentations that shed light

on the city's past, including its rise, glory, and eventual downfall.

3.2 Ayutthaya Elephant Palace and Royal Kraal:
Located near the historical park, the Ayutthaya Elephant Palace and Royal Kraal provides a unique opportunity to interact with these majestic creatures. Visitors can learn about the importance of elephants in Thai culture, witness captivating shows, and even take an elephant ride around the park.

3.3 Ayutthaya Floating Market:
Immerse yourself in the vibrant atmosphere of the Ayutthaya Floating Market, where you can experience traditional Thai market culture. Browse through a variety of stalls offering local handicrafts, fresh produce, and delectable street food. Take a boat ride along the canal, savoring the picturesque scenery and enjoying the lively ambiance.

Practical Information and Tips:

4.1 Getting There:
Ayutthaya is conveniently located around 80 kilometers north of Bangkok, making it easily accessible by various means of transportation.

Travelers can opt for a short train ride from Bangkok's Hua Lamphong Station, a bus journey, or even a private tour.

4.2 Exploring the Park:
To make the most of your visit to Ayutthaya Historical Park, consider renting a bicycle or hiring a tuk-tuk driver who can navigate the vast area efficiently. Remember to bring sunscreen, a hat, and comfortable footwear, as exploring the park involves considerable walking or cycling.

4.3 Dress Code and Respect:
As Ayutthaya is a religious site, it is important to dress modestly and respectfully. Both men and women should ensure their shoulders and knees are covered when entering temples or sacred areas.

A trip to Ayutthaya Historical Park is a journey through time, offering a glimpse into Thailand's magnificent past. The remnants of this once-mighty city evoke a sense of awe and wonder, inviting travelers to discover the stories etched within its ancient walls. From majestic temples to fascinating ruins, Ayutthaya stands as a testament to the enduring spirit of the Thai people and their rich cultural heritage. As you explore the park and its surroundings, you will find yourself captivated by the grandeur and serenity that pervades every corner. Ayutthaya is undoubtedly a must-visit destination for any traveler seeking to immerse themselves in Thailand's fascinating history.

•*Sukhothai Historical Park*

Thailand, known for its rich cultural heritage and breathtaking landscapes, offers a myriad of fascinating attractions for travelers. One such gem is the Sukhothai Historical Park, located in the northern part of the country. With its ancient ruins, serene surroundings, and historical significance, Sukhothai Historical Park is a must-visit destination for history enthusiasts and avid travelers alike. In this comprehensive travel guide, we will delve into the historical significance of the park, explore its notable attractions, provide practical travel tips, and showcase the best ways to make the most of your visit.

I. Unveiling the Historical Significance:
Sukhothai Historical Park, a UNESCO World Heritage Site, holds immense historical importance as the capital of the Kingdom of Sukhothai from the 13th to the 15th centuries. This period is regarded as the golden age of Thai civilization, marking the birth of the Thai nation. The park showcases the remnants of this prosperous era, where art, architecture, and religion flourished.

II. Exploring the Park's Highlights:

Central Zone:
The central zone serves as the heart of the Sukhothai Historical Park, housing numerous ancient temples, stupas, and other significant structures. Notable attractions in this zone include the iconic Wat Mahathat, Wat Si Sawai, and Wat Traphang Ngoen, which provide insight into the architectural grandeur and religious beliefs of the ancient Sukhothai kingdom.

Northern Zone:
The northern zone of the park features several well-preserved temples, including Wat Phra Phai Luang and Wat Si Chum. The majestic Buddha statue at Wat Si Chum, known as Phra

Achana, is a highlight of this zone. The serenity and tranquility of the northern zone make it an ideal place for contemplation and spiritual reflection.

Western Zone:
The western zone is home to some of the most iconic and picturesque ruins in the park. Notable temples in this area include Wat Saphan Hin and Wat Chetuphon, offering panoramic views of the surrounding landscape. Visitors can also explore the Ramkhamhaeng National Museum, which provides a deeper understanding of the historical and cultural context of the park.

III. Practical Travel Tips:

Best Time to Visit:
The ideal time to visit Sukhothai Historical Park is during the cool and dry season from November to February. The weather during this period is pleasant, allowing visitors to explore the park comfortably. Avoid visiting during the rainy season (June to October) when heavy downpours can hinder outdoor activities.

Getting There:

Sukhothai has its own airport, making it easily accessible from major cities like Bangkok and Chiang Mai. Alternatively, visitors can opt for a train or bus journey to Sukhothai. Once in the city, the historical park is just a short distance away and can be reached by local transportation or rented bicycles.

Entrance Fees and Opening Hours:
The park's entrance fee is nominal and allows access to all zones. The opening hours are from 6:00 AM to 6:00 PM, ensuring ample time for exploration and photography. Consider arriving early in the morning to witness the sunrise casting a mesmerizing glow over the ancient ruins.

Exploring the Park:
Renting bicycles within the park is a popular and convenient way to explore the extensive grounds. Bicycles can be rented near the entrance, and cycling allows visitors to cover more ground while enjoying the scenic beauty of the surroundings. Electric tram tours are also available for those who prefer a leisurely guided experience.

Dress Code and Etiquette:

As Sukhothai Historical Park is a sacred site, it is important to dress modestly and respectfully. Visitors should avoid wearing revealing clothing and should cover their shoulders and knees. Removing shoes before entering temple structures is customary, and visitors should be mindful of their behavior and avoid touching or damaging the ancient ruins.

IV. Beyond the Historical Park:

Sukhothai Town:
Exploring the charming town of Sukhothai is a delightful experience. The Old City area offers a glimpse into traditional Thai architecture and houses various local markets, where visitors can sample authentic Thai cuisine and purchase handmade crafts and souvenirs.

Si Satchanalai Historical Park:
For those with an appetite for more historical wonders, a visit to the nearby Si Satchanalai Historical Park is highly recommended. This park showcases the ruins of another ancient city from the Sukhothai period and provides a deeper understanding of the region's historical significance.

Sukhothai Historical Park stands as a testament to Thailand's glorious past and offers a remarkable journey back in time. With its awe-inspiring ruins, serene ambiance, and cultural significance, the park captivates visitors from around the world. By following this comprehensive travel guide, you can make the most of your visit to Sukhothai Historical Park, ensuring a memorable and enriching experience that will leave you in awe of Thailand's rich heritage.

- ### *Wat Phra Mahathat in Nakhon Si Thammarat*

Thailand, known for its rich cultural heritage and stunning temples, is a treasure trove for travelers seeking an immersive experience. Among its numerous architectural marvels, Wat Phra Mahathat in Nakhon Si Thammarat stands out as a symbol of spiritual grandeur and historical significance. This ancient temple, dating back over seven centuries, is a testament to Thailand's enduring Buddhist tradition. In this comprehensive Thailand travel guide, we will delve into the captivating allure of Wat Phra Mahathat, exploring its history, architectural features, cultural significance, and practical travel information.

I. Historical Background :
Wat Phra Mahathat holds deep historical roots that trace back to the 13th century. It was established during the reign of King Sri Thammasokarat, making it one of the oldest temples in Thailand. The temple played a crucial role in spreading Theravada Buddhism and acted as the principal learning center for Buddhist teachings in southern Thailand.

II. Architectural Splendor :
The temple's architectural style blends elements of Sukhothai and Srivijaya influences, reflecting the region's cultural and historical connections. The most iconic feature of Wat Phra Mahathat is its towering central pagoda, known as the Phra Borommathat Chedi. This majestic structure, adorned with intricate carvings and gilded ornaments, rises to a height of 78 meters, making it one of the tallest pagodas in Thailand. Visitors can climb the steps to the top, where panoramic views of the city and surrounding landscapes await.

Surrounding the central pagoda are numerous smaller chedis, each housing relics and treasures. These smaller chedis showcase diverse architectural styles and intricate detailing, providing a visual feast for visitors. The temple complex also includes several viharas (assembly halls), where devotees and monks gather for prayers and religious ceremonies.

III. Cultural Significance:

Wat Phra Mahathat holds immense cultural significance for the Thai people, particularly those practicing Theravada Buddhism. The temple is renowned as one of the holiest sites in southern Thailand, attracting both locals and pilgrims from afar. Its historical importance as a center for Buddhist education has earned it the esteemed status of Mahavihara, signifying its role as a prominent monastic institution.

The temple is home to an important relic—the Buddha's tooth. Encased within the Phra Borommathat Chedi, this relic is believed to possess sacred power and draws devout Buddhists who seek blessings and spiritual solace. Additionally, the temple complex houses a museum that displays a remarkable collection of artifacts, statues, and religious manuscripts, offering visitors a glimpse into Thailand's rich cultural heritage.

IV. Experiencing Wat Phra Mahathat :

Meditation and Spiritual Practices:
Wat Phra Mahathat offers visitors an opportunity to immerse themselves in the serene ambiance and engage in spiritual practices. The temple provides meditation retreats and workshops, allowing participants to learn meditation techniques under the guidance of experienced monks. These programs offer a chance to explore inner peace and gain insights into Buddhist philosophy.

Cultural Festivals and Events:
To witness the vibrant cultural traditions associated with Wat Phra Mahathat, visitors should plan their visit during significant festivals. One such event is the Phra Phuttha Sihing Buddha Image Procession, held annually in May. During this grand procession, a revered Buddha image is paraded through the streets of Nakhon Si Thammarat, attracting a multitude of locals and tourists.

Exploring the Surroundings:

Beyond the temple's spiritual aspects, the surrounding area offers additional attractions. Nearby, the Old Town of Nakhon Si Thammarat presents an opportunity to explore historic buildings, traditional markets, and local cuisine. The shadow puppetry performances and traditional dance shows are not to be missed.

Practical Information :

Wat Phra Mahathat is located in Nakhon Si Thammarat, approximately 780 kilometers south of Bangkok.

The temple is open daily from 8:00 am to 5:00 pm, and admission is free, though donations are appreciated.

Modest attire is required, with shoulders and knees covered as a sign of respect.

Photography is permitted within the temple complex, but it is advised to be mindful of others' privacy and religious practices.

English signage and audio guides are available, providing visitors with historical and cultural insights.

Local guides can be hired to gain a deeper understanding of the temple's significance.

Accommodations ranging from budget to luxury can be found in Nakhon Si Thammarat, catering to various traveler preferences.

A journey to Thailand would be incomplete without experiencing the awe-inspiring beauty and tranquility of Wat Phra Mahathat in Nakhon Si Thammarat. This ancient temple, with its rich history, architectural splendor, and cultural significance, is a testament to Thailand's enduring devotion to Buddhism. Whether you seek spiritual enlightenment, cultural immersion, or architectural marvels, Wat Phra Mahathat offers an enchanting experience that will leave an indelible impression on your soul. Embrace the serenity, witness the vibrant traditions, and unravel the mysteries of this timeless gem in the heart of Thailand.

•The Bridge over the River Kwai in Kanchanaburi

Located in the charming town of Kanchanaburi, Thailand, the Bridge over the

River Kwai stands as a poignant testament to the dark and turbulent history of World War II. This iconic landmark has not only become a significant historical site but also a major tourist attraction, drawing visitors from all around the world. In this Thailand travel guide, we will delve into the rich history of the Bridge over the River Kwai, explore its cultural significance, and provide you with essential information to make the most of your visit.

Historical Background
The construction of the Bridge over the River Kwai is closely linked to the infamous "Death Railway" built by the Japanese during World War II. The railway aimed to connect Thailand with Burma (now Myanmar) to support the Japanese war effort. It was constructed using forced labor, including prisoners of war and Asian laborers, under grueling conditions.

The bridge itself, officially known as the Mae Klong Bridge, spans the River Kwai Yai and was a crucial part of the railway line. Its construction commenced in 1942 and was completed in 1943. The bridge gained international recognition through Pierre Boulle's novel, "The Bridge over the River

Kwai," and later the Oscar-winning film adaptation.

The Bridge Today

The Bridge over the River Kwai still stands proudly as a symbol of resilience and survival. The original wooden structure was replaced with a steel bridge after the war, but it maintains the architectural style of the original construction. Visitors can walk across the bridge, witnessing the picturesque views of the river and surrounding landscapes.

The bridge has undergone several renovations and restorations over the years, ensuring its preservation for future generations. Today, it serves as a memorial and museum, providing valuable insights into the historical significance of the Death Railway and the suffering endured by those involved in its construction.

The Death Railway Museum

Adjacent to the Bridge over the River Kwai is the Death Railway Museum, a must-visit for anyone interested in delving deeper into the history of this harrowing period. The museum showcases a comprehensive collection of artifacts, photographs, and personal accounts that shed light on the events surrounding the construction of the railway and the experiences of the prisoners of war.

Visitors can explore the museum's exhibits, which depict the hardships faced by the laborers, the brutal treatment endured, and the impact the railway had on the local communities. The museum offers a somber and thought-provoking experience, allowing visitors to reflect on the atrocities of war and honor the memory of those who lost their lives.

Exploring Kanchanaburi

Beyond the Bridge over the River Kwai, Kanchanaburi boasts a range of attractions that should not be missed. The town is surrounded by lush landscapes, including national parks, waterfalls, and historical sites. The Erawan National Park, with its magnificent seven-tiered waterfall, offers a perfect escape into nature. Visitors can also explore the Hellfire Pass Memorial Museum, which commemorates the thousands who perished while constructing this treacherous section of the Death Railway.

Additionally, the JEATH War Museum provides further insight into the history of the Death Railway, showcasing replicas of the bamboo huts that prisoners of war lived in during their captivity. The museum displays photographs, tools, and other artifacts, giving visitors a glimpse into the lives of those who suffered through unimaginable conditions.

A visit to the Bridge over the River Kwai in Kanchanaburi is a journey back in time, allowing visitors to pay tribute to the lives lost during one of the darkest chapters in human history. As a symbol of resilience and survival, the bridge serves as a stark reminder of the sacrifices made during World War II. Combined with the compelling exhibits at the Death Railway Museum and the exploration of Kanchanaburi's other historical and natural attractions, this destination offers a unique blend of education, reflection, and natural beauty.

CHAPTER EIGHT

Shopping and Markets

• *Night Bazaars and Night Markets*

Thailand, known as the "Land of Smiles," is a captivating destination that offers a diverse range of experiences for travelers. Among its many attractions, the country's night bazaars and night markets stand out as vibrant hubs of activity, filled with an abundance of sights, sounds, and flavors. In this comprehensive Thailand travel guide, we will delve into the enchanting world of night bazaars and night markets, providing you with insights into their history, must-visit locations across the country, and tips for navigating these bustling nocturnal havens.

The Origins and Significance of Night Bazaars and Night Markets:
Night bazaars and night markets have been an integral part of Thai culture for centuries. These vibrant gatherings evolved from

traditional markets and trade routes, where villagers and merchants would gather to exchange goods and socialize. Over time, they transformed into bustling nocturnal marketplaces, offering a unique blend of commerce, entertainment, and local culture.

The Allure of Night Bazaars and Night Markets in Thailand:

a. Vibrant Shopping Experience: Night bazaars and night markets in Thailand are a shopaholic's paradise, with a vast array of products on offer. From clothing, accessories, and handicrafts to electronics, souvenirs, and antiques, these markets cater to all tastes and budgets. Talad Rot Fai Ratchada in Bangkok, Chiang Mai Night Bazaar, and Phuket Weekend Market are among the most popular shopping destinations.

b. Culinary Delights: Thailand is renowned for its delectable street food, and night bazaars and night markets are ideal places to savor authentic local dishes. Explore the tantalizing world of Thai cuisine, from savory Pad Thai and spicy Tom Yum Goong to grilled skewers, fresh seafood, and sweet mango sticky rice.

c. Cultural Immersion: Immerse yourself in the rich cultural tapestry of Thailand through its night markets. Engage with friendly locals, witness traditional performances, and browse through stalls selling traditional arts and crafts. You might even stumble upon local festivities or live music performances, adding to the vibrant atmosphere.

d. Bargaining Thrills: Negotiating prices is a customary practice in Thai markets. Hone your bargaining skills and engage in friendly banter with the vendors. While not all items can be bargained for, it adds an element of excitement and can result in fantastic deals and memorable experiences.

Unmissable Night Bazaars and Night Markets across Thailand:

a. Bangkok:

i. Talad Rot Fai Ratchada: Located in the Ratchada neighborhood, this sprawling market offers a unique blend of vintage collectibles, fashion, and trendy eateries. With a lively atmosphere, it's a perfect spot for shopping enthusiasts and food lovers alike.

ii. Patpong Night Market: Situated in the heart of Bangkok's entertainment district, Patpong

Night Market is famous for its lively nightlife, knock-off designer goods, and vibrant street performances.

b. Chiang Mai:
i. Chiang Mai Night Bazaar: This iconic market is a treasure trove of handicrafts, textiles, and local artwork. Explore the maze of stalls, and don't miss the opportunity to sample traditional Northern Thai cuisine.

ii. Sunday Walking Street: Taking place every Sunday evening, this market stretches along the ancient city walls of Chiang Mai. It showcases an extensive range of unique handicrafts, artistic creations, and live performances.

c. Phuket:
i. Phuket Weekend Market (Naka Market): A bustling market that comes alive every weekend, offering a diverse range of products, from clothing and accessories to electronics and street food. Take your time to explore the maze of stalls and indulge in local delicacies.

ii. Malin Plaza Patong: Located in Patong Beach, this vibrant night market is known for its lively atmosphere, live music performances, and delectable street food options. It's an ideal spot to immerse yourself in the local culture while enjoying a lively evening out.

Tips for Exploring Night Bazaars and Night Markets:

a. Go Early: Arriving early allows you to beat the crowds and have a more relaxed shopping experience. It also gives you a chance to witness the market come alive as the sun sets.

b. Dress Comfortably: Wear light, breathable clothing and comfortable footwear, as you'll be walking and exploring for hours.

c. Stay Hydrated: Night markets can be hot and humid, so carry a water bottle to stay hydrated throughout your visit.

d. Be Adventurous with Food: Night markets offer an excellent opportunity to sample a wide variety of Thai street food. Be adventurous and try new dishes, but also ensure that the food is prepared hygienically.

e. Practice Bargaining: Negotiating prices is part of the culture in Thai markets. Approach bargaining with a friendly attitude and be prepared to walk away if the price doesn't suit your budget.

f. Stay Alert and Mindful: Night markets can be crowded, so keep an eye on your belongings and be cautious of pickpockets. Stay aware of your surroundings and trust your instincts.

Night bazaars and night markets in Thailand are a kaleidoscope of colors, aromas, and cultural experiences. These vibrant marketplaces offer a glimpse into the heart and soul of Thai life, and exploring them is an essential part of any visit to this captivating country. Whether you're seeking unique souvenirs, mouthwatering street food, or an opportunity to immerse yourself in local culture, Thailand's night bazaars and night markets will leave you with unforgettable memories of your journey through the Land of Smiles.

•CentralWorld in Bangkok

CentralWorld, located in the heart of Bangkok, Thailand, is a world-renowned shopping and entertainment complex that epitomizes the city's vibrant and dynamic lifestyle. Spanning an impressive area of over 550,000 square meters, CentralWorld is one of the largest shopping centers in the world and a must-visit destination for both locals and tourists. Boasting an extensive range of retail outlets, exquisite dining options, exciting entertainment facilities, and a prime location, CentralWorld offers an unforgettable experience that captures the essence of Bangkok's cosmopolitan charm.

History and Development

CentralWorld traces its roots back to 1990 when the Central Group, one of Thailand's leading retail conglomerates, embarked on an ambitious project to create a revolutionary shopping complex. The development of CentralWorld began in 2002, and the grand opening took place in 2006. It was a significant milestone for Bangkok's retail landscape, introducing a new era of retail experiences.

Iconic Features and Design

CentralWorld's architectural marvel is a sight to behold. The complex features a contemporary design with sleek lines, glass facades, and modern aesthetics. The iconic centerpiece is the magnificent CentralWorld Square, a vast outdoor plaza that hosts various events, concerts, and festivals throughout the year. The square serves as a focal point for visitors and adds to the lively atmosphere of the complex.

Shopping Extravaganza

CentralWorld offers an unparalleled shopping experience with an extensive range of stores catering to every taste and budget. From high-end luxury brands to popular international retailers, fashion boutiques, electronics, home decor, cosmetics, and more, the complex has it all. Anchored by flagship department stores like Central Department Store and Zen Department Store, shoppers can explore multiple floors filled with fashion, accessories, beauty products, and lifestyle goods.

Gastronomic Delights

CentralWorld is a food lover's paradise, with an array of dining options that cater to diverse palates. From local Thai delicacies to international cuisines, the complex houses numerous restaurants, cafes, and food courts. Visitors can indulge in authentic Thai street food, savor gourmet dishes from renowned chefs, or enjoy a cup of coffee at trendy cafes. Whether you're looking for a quick bite or a fine dining experience, CentralWorld offers a culinary adventure for all.

Entertainment and Leisure

Beyond shopping and dining, CentralWorld provides an abundance of entertainment and leisure activities. The complex is home to a world-class cinema, offering the latest blockbusters and international films. For thrill-seekers, there is an indoor ice skating rink that provides a refreshing break from the tropical heat. Additionally, visitors can challenge themselves at the popular Bounce Trampoline Park, which offers an exhilarating experience for both children and adults alike.

Cultural and Artistic Experiences

CentralWorld embraces Thai culture and regularly hosts cultural events, exhibitions, and art showcases. The complex features art galleries that display contemporary Thai art, providing a platform for local artists to showcase their talent. Visitors can immerse themselves in the rich cultural heritage of Thailand through traditional performances, exhibitions, and workshops held within the complex.

Location and Accessibility

Situated in Bangkok's bustling Ratchaprasong district, CentralWorld enjoys a prime location that is easily accessible. It is conveniently connected to the Chidlom BTS Skytrain station via a skywalk, providing seamless transportation for visitors. The complex is also in close proximity to other popular attractions like Siam Paragon, MBK Center, and Erawan Shrine, making it an ideal destination for a full day of exploration.

CentralWorld is an iconic landmark in Bangkok, offering an extraordinary blend of shopping, dining, entertainment, and cultural experiences. With its sheer size, diverse offerings, and prime location, it has become an integral part of Bangkok's cosmopolitan landscape. A visit to CentralWorld is an opportunity to immerse oneself in the vibrant energy of the city, indulge in retail therapy, sample delectable cuisines, and appreciate the artistic expressions of Thailand. For travelers seeking a comprehensive and unforgettable experience in Bangkok, CentralWorld stands as an essential destination not to be missed.

•Walking Streets and Weekend Markets

Thailand is renowned for its rich cultural heritage, vibrant markets, and bustling streets that come alive during the weekends. Among the many attractions, Walking Streets and Weekend Markets hold a special place in the hearts of locals and tourists alike. These lively marketplaces offer a unique opportunity to experience the essence of Thailand, with their vibrant atmosphere, diverse street food, traditional handicrafts, and lively entertainment. In this Thailand travel guide, we will delve into the enchanting world of Walking Streets and Weekend Markets, providing you with insights into some of the most popular and captivating markets across the country.

Walking Streets: A Cultural Extravaganza

Walking Streets, also known as walking markets or night markets, are a distinctive Thai phenomenon that showcases the country's rich cultural heritage and local traditions. These markets typically take place in pedestrianized streets, allowing visitors to explore and immerse themselves in a vibrant and bustling atmosphere. Here are some renowned Walking Streets in Thailand:

1.1. Chiang Mai Walking Street

Located in the heart of the charming city of Chiang Mai, the Chiang Mai Walking Street is a paradise for art enthusiasts and souvenir collectors. It stretches for nearly one kilometer and is lined with stalls offering a wide range of handicrafts, artwork, clothing, and local delicacies. Visitors can witness traditional dance performances, live music, and indulge in delectable street food as they navigate through the colorful streets.

1.2. Khao San Road in Bangkok

Khao San Road, situated in the vibrant city of Bangkok, is renowned for its bustling atmosphere and lively street life. Although not a traditional Walking Street, it offers a similar experience with its abundance of stalls selling clothes, accessories, and souvenirs. The street also boasts a vibrant nightlife scene, with numerous bars, clubs, and restaurants catering to the diverse tastes of travelers from around the world.

1.3. Walking Street in Pattaya
Pattaya's Walking Street is an iconic destination renowned for its energetic nightlife and vibrant entertainment options. Stretching for approximately 500 meters, this pedestrianized street comes alive after sunset, offering a sensory overload of neon lights, music, and bustling crowds. The street is dotted with street food stalls, bars, nightclubs, and even muay Thai boxing matches, making it a must-visit attraction for those seeking an exhilarating experience in Thailand.

Weekend Markets: A Shopper's Paradise

Thailand's weekend markets are a shopaholic's delight, offering an incredible array of merchandise, from fashion and accessories to handicrafts and antiques. These markets provide a glimpse into the local way of life and are a treasure trove for unique souvenirs. Here are some notable weekend markets in Thailand:

2.1. Chatuchak Weekend Market in Bangkok

Chatuchak Weekend Market, also known as JJ Market, is one of the largest and most famous markets in Southeast Asia. Covering an expansive area of 35 acres, it hosts over 15,000 stalls offering a staggering variety of goods, including clothing, home decor, plants, antiques, and street food. Navigating through its labyrinthine alleys is an adventure in itself, and visitors can easily spend hours exploring the market's vibrant sections dedicated to art, fashion, pets, and more.

2.2. Chiang Mai's Sunday Night Market

Chiang Mai's Sunday Night Market is a vibrant showcase of the city's cultural heritage and artistic traditions. Held in the old town area, the market is a haven for handicraft enthusiasts, offering an extensive range of locally made products such as textiles, ceramics, woodwork, and silverware. The market's lively atmosphere is further enhanced by traditional performances, live music, and street food stalls serving mouthwatering Northern Thai delicacies.

2.3. Walking Street Market in Hua Hin

Located along the picturesque seaside town of Hua Hin, the Walking Street Market is a charming destination for both locals and tourists. This lively market offers a delightful mix of clothing, accessories, handmade crafts, and delicious street food. Visitors can also find unique souvenirs, such as seashell jewelry and hand-painted ceramics, reflecting the coastal vibe of the town. The market's proximity to the beach makes it an ideal spot for enjoying the sunset while savoring delectable snacks from the various food stalls.

The Enchanting Experience
Visiting Thailand's Walking Streets and Weekend Markets is not just about shopping; it's an immersive cultural experience that allows travelers to interact with locals, sample traditional cuisine, and appreciate the country's artistic and culinary heritage. Here are some tips to enhance your experience:

3.1. Arrive Early
To beat the crowds and have a more relaxed shopping experience, consider visiting the markets early in the day, especially if you're interested in rare finds or limited-edition items.

3.2. Bargain with a Smile
Haggling is a common practice in Thai markets, so don't hesitate to negotiate the price. Approach it with a friendly attitude, and

you may find yourself getting a good deal while engaging in lighthearted banter with the vendors.

3.3. Try Local Delicacies
One of the highlights of these markets is the diverse street food offerings. Be adventurous and sample local delicacies like pad Thai, mango sticky rice, and grilled skewers. Don't forget to indulge in refreshing drinks like coconut water or Thai iced tea.

Thailand's Walking Streets and Weekend Markets offer an enchanting blend of culture, shopping, and culinary delights. Whether you're seeking traditional handicrafts, mouthwatering street food, or simply want to immerse yourself in the lively atmosphere, these markets provide an authentic glimpse into Thai life. From the bustling streets of Bangkok to the charming markets of Chiang Mai and Pattaya, the country's vibrant marketplaces are a must-visit for any traveler seeking a memorable experience in the Land of Smiles.

•Floating Markets

Thailand, renowned for its vibrant culture and rich heritage, offers visitors an array of unforgettable experiences. Among its many treasures, the floating markets stand out as unique and captivating attractions. These lively marketplaces, nestled along the country's extensive network of canals and rivers, provide a glimpse into Thailand's traditional way of life while offering an exciting shopping and culinary adventure. In this comprehensive travel guide, we will delve into the enchanting world of Thailand's floating markets, highlighting their history, significance, top destinations, activities, and essential tips for an unforgettable visit.

I. History and Significance of Floating Markets

Thailand's floating markets have a deep-rooted history dating back to the time when rivers and canals were the primary means of transportation. These markets served as vital trading hubs, where locals would gather to sell and exchange goods, creating a vibrant economic center. They played a crucial role in connecting communities and sustaining the livelihoods of the people living along the waterways.

II. Top Floating Markets in Thailand

a) Damnoen Saduak Floating Market: Located near Bangkok, Damnoen Saduak is perhaps the most famous floating market in Thailand. Its bustling atmosphere, vibrant boat vendors, and diverse range of goods make it a must-visit destination.

b) Amphawa Floating Market: Situated in Samut Songkhram province, Amphawa offers an authentic and less touristy floating market experience. Visitors can explore its charming canals, sample local delicacies, and witness the mesmerizing sight of hundreds of lanterns illuminating the water at night.

c) Taling Chan Floating Market: Conveniently located within Bangkok's city limits, Taling Chan is a popular choice for both locals and tourists seeking a delightful floating market experience. Here, visitors can enjoy fresh seafood, indulge in Thai desserts, and even take a longtail boat tour of the nearby orchid farms.

d) Khlong Lat Mayom Floating Market: Located on the outskirts of Bangkok, Khlong Lat Mayom is known for its picturesque setting and laid-back ambiance. Visitors can savor an array of delectable dishes, shop for handicrafts, and immerse themselves in the natural beauty of the nearby orchards and gardens.

III. Activities and Experiences

a) Boat Tours: Exploring the canals and waterways by boat is an essential part of the floating market experience. Visitors can hire a traditional longtail boat or join guided tours to navigate the intricate network of water channels, witness local life along the banks, and discover hidden gems.

b) Shopping: Floating markets offer a cornucopia of goods, ranging from fresh produce, tropical fruits, and vegetables to handicrafts, clothing, and souvenirs. Bargaining is an integral part of the shopping experience, so visitors should embrace their haggling skills to secure the best deals.

c) Culinary Delights: The floating markets are a food lover's paradise, with countless stalls and boats offering tantalizing Thai street food. Visitors can savor iconic dishes like pad Thai, tom yum soup, mango sticky rice, and freshly grilled seafood, all prepared with authentic flavors and local ingredients.

d) Cultural Performances: Some floating markets showcase traditional Thai cultural performances, including music, dance, and puppet shows. These captivating displays provide a deeper understanding of Thailand's artistic heritage and add an extra layer of enchantment to the market experience.

IV. Practical Tips for Visiting Floating Markets

a) Best Time to Visit: Floating markets are typically more vibrant in the mornings, so it's advisable to arrive early to beat the crowds and enjoy a more authentic atmosphere.

b) Getting There: Most floating markets are easily accessible from major cities like Bangkok. Visitors can choose between public buses, private taxis, or organized tours, depending on their preferences.

c) Dress Code: As with any temple or cultural site in Thailand, it is respectful to dress modestly when visiting floating markets. Light, comfortable clothing and appropriate footwear are recommended.

d) Cash and Small Change: It's advisable to carry enough cash, preferably in smaller denominations, as many vendors may not accept credit cards or larger bills. ATMs are usually available nearby.

e) Hydration and Sun Protection: Thailand's tropical climate can be hot and humid, so it's crucial to stay hydrated and apply sunscreen regularly. Carrying a reusable water bottle and wearing a hat and sunglasses are recommended.

Thailand's floating markets offer a magical blend of history, culture, and sensory delights, providing an experience unlike any other. Exploring these lively marketplaces allows visitors to immerse themselves in the traditional way of life, taste authentic flavors, and witness the vibrant tapestry of Thai culture. From the iconic Damnoen Saduak to the off-the-beaten-path Amphawa and beyond, each floating market has its unique charm and offerings. By following this comprehensive travel guide, visitors can make the most of their journey, create lasting memories, and embark on an unforgettable adventure through the captivating world of Thailand's floating markets.

CHAPTER NINE

Thai Spa and Wellness

• *Traditional Thai Massage*

Thailand, known for its rich cultural heritage and warm hospitality, offers a wide range of experiences for travelers. One such experience that stands out is Traditional Thai Massage. Rooted in ancient healing traditions and practiced for centuries, Thai massage is a therapeutic art form that combines elements of acupressure, yoga, and meditation. In this comprehensive Thailand travel guide, we will delve into the fascinating world of Traditional Thai Massage, exploring its history, techniques, health benefits, and where to experience this rejuvenating practice in Thailand.

I. Historical Background

Thai massage, also known as Nuad Thai, has a long and intricate history dating back over 2,500 years. Its origins can be traced to India, where Ayurvedic practices and Buddhist teachings heavily influenced Thai culture. Thai massage was initially practiced by Buddhist monks as a way to promote physical and spiritual well-being. Over time, it evolved into a holistic healing system passed down through generations.

II. The Art of Traditional Thai Massage

A. Techniques and Principles: Traditional Thai Massage combines acupressure, passive stretching, and applied yoga postures. Practitioners use their hands, thumbs, elbows, knees, and feet to apply pressure along energy lines, known as "Sen," which are believed to run through the body. The massage is performed on a floor mat, with the recipient fully clothed in loose, comfortable attire.

B. Benefits of Thai Massage: Thai massage offers numerous benefits, including stress reduction, increased flexibility, improved circulation, enhanced energy flow, and relief from muscular tension. It promotes overall well-being and harmony between the mind, body, and spirit.

III. Experiencing Traditional Thai Massage in Thailand

A. Bangkok: As the bustling capital of Thailand, Bangkok is a treasure trove for Traditional Thai Massage enthusiasts. Notable places to experience Thai massage include Wat Pho, home to the world-famous Wat Pho Massage School, and upscale spas like The Oriental Spa and Banyan Tree Spa.

B. Chiang Mai: Known as the cultural hub of Northern Thailand, Chiang Mai offers an authentic and serene setting for Thai massage. The Old City is replete with massage centers and wellness retreats, including the renowned Namo Spa and Fah Lanna Spa.

C. Phuket: Thailand's largest island, Phuket, offers a tranquil escape for indulging in Thai massage. Patong Beach and Kata Beach are popular areas with a myriad of massage parlors and spas, such as Let's Relax Spa and Oasis Spa.

D. Other Regions: Thai massage is practiced throughout the country, and each region offers unique experiences. In Pattaya, visitors can enjoy massage treatments by the beach, while in Krabi, they can find solace in luxurious resorts like Rayavadee Spa. Additionally, the islands of Koh Samui and Koh Phi Phi are known for their idyllic spa retreats.

IV. Etiquette and Tips for Thai Massage

A. Attire: Traditional Thai Massage is typically performed with the recipient fully clothed, so it is advisable to wear loose and comfortable clothing.

B. Communication: Clear communication with the massage therapist is essential to ensure a tailored experience. Discuss any specific concerns, preferences, or health conditions before the session begins.

C. Respect for Tradition: Thai massage is deeply rooted in Thai culture and traditions. Respecting the therapist and the sacred nature of the practice is important. Remaining calm, relaxed, and refraining from disruptive behavior is highly appreciated.

V. Precautions and Contraindications (200 words)
While Thai massage is generally safe and beneficial, certain precautions should be taken. It is advisable to consult with a healthcare professional if you have any pre-existing medical conditions. Pregnant women,

individuals with open wounds, recent surgeries, or severe osteoporosis should exercise caution and inform the therapist beforehand.

•*Wellness Retreats and Spa Resorts*

Thailand, renowned for its vibrant culture, stunning landscapes, and warm hospitality, is also a sought-after destination for wellness retreats and spa resorts. Offering a perfect blend of traditional healing practices and modern wellness amenities, Thailand caters to the needs of travelers seeking relaxation, rejuvenation, and holistic well-being. From luxurious resorts nestled amidst tranquil natural surroundings to urban sanctuaries in bustling cities, Thailand presents an array of options for those yearning to escape the stresses of daily life. In this comprehensive travel guide, we will explore the essence of wellness retreats and spa resorts in Thailand, highlighting the unique experiences, rejuvenating treatments, and cultural influences that make them an ideal choice for wellness enthusiasts.

I. The Essence of Wellness Retreats in Thailand :

A. Traditional Healing Practices: Thai wellness retreats draw inspiration from ancient healing traditions such as Ayurveda, Traditional Chinese Medicine, and Thai traditional medicine. These retreats emphasize a holistic approach to wellness, focusing on physical, mental, and spiritual well-being.

B. Tranquil Natural Settings: Nestled amidst breathtaking landscapes, wellness retreats in Thailand provide an idyllic environment for relaxation and rejuvenation. From pristine beaches and lush jungles to serene mountains and riverside retreats, each location offers a unique ambiance for unwinding and connecting with nature.

C. Mindfulness and Meditation: Wellness retreats in Thailand often incorporate mindfulness and meditation practices, enabling guests to cultivate inner peace and enhance self-awareness. Experienced instructors guide participants through meditation sessions, breathing exercises, and mindfulness workshops, fostering a sense of calm and balance.

D. Healthy Cuisine: Nourishing the body is an integral part of wellness retreats. Thailand's culinary traditions, renowned for their emphasis on fresh ingredients, aromatic herbs, and spices, offer a delectable range of healthy and nutritious options. Guests can savor a variety of organic, vegetarian, and vegan dishes tailored to support their wellness journey.

II. Spa Resorts: A Haven of Relaxation:
A. Luxurious Accommodations: Spa resorts in Thailand boast opulent accommodations, combining Thai aesthetics with modern comforts. From private villas with plunge pools to spacious suites overlooking panoramic views, these resorts provide a serene sanctuary for guests to unwind and rejuvenate.

B. Signature Spa Treatments: Thai spa resorts are celebrated for their exceptional spa treatments that blend traditional techniques with contemporary innovations. Guests can indulge in ancient Thai massages, herbal therapies, aromatherapy, and unique rituals designed to promote relaxation, detoxification, and restoration.

C. Thermal Facilities and Hydrotherapy: Many spa resorts feature thermal facilities such as saunas, steam rooms, and hot springs, allowing guests to detoxify and revitalize their bodies. Hydrotherapy pools and whirlpools offer therapeutic benefits, while cold plunge pools invigorate the senses and enhance circulation.

D. Wellness Activities and Fitness: Spa resorts in Thailand provide a range of wellness activities and fitness programs to cater to guests' preferences. Yoga and Pilates classes, guided nature walks, tai chi sessions, and water sports enable visitors to maintain an active lifestyle and discover inner balance.

III. Popular Wellness Retreats and Spa Resorts in Thailand :

A. Chiva-Som International Health Resort (Hua Hin): Renowned for its comprehensive wellness programs and holistic approach, Chiva-Som offers personalized retreats focusing on detoxification, stress management, weight loss, and rejuvenation. Its tranquil beachfront location and luxurious facilities make it a preferred destination for wellness seekers worldwide.

B. Kamalaya Koh Samui (Koh Samui): Nestled amidst a tropical paradise, Kamalaya combines traditional healing practices with modern therapies. Guests can partake in yoga, meditation, and qigong sessions, as well as indulge in diverse spa treatments and wellness consultations.

C. Anantara Golden Triangle Elephant Camp & Resort (Chiang Rai): Set in the enchanting Golden Triangle region, this unique resort allows guests to experience wellness while interacting with elephants. Guests can enjoy spa treatments, yoga, and mindfulness sessions, as well as elephant encounters and mahout training programs.

D. Four Seasons Resort Chiang Mai (Chiang Mai): Surrounded by lush rice paddies and mountains, this luxurious resort offers an array of wellness activities, including yoga, Thai boxing, and traditional spa therapies. The resort's renowned cooking school also provides guests with culinary insights into healthy Thai cuisine.

E. Banyan Tree Phuket (Phuket): With its serene location on the shores of the Andaman Sea, Banyan Tree Phuket is a tranquil oasis offering rejuvenating spa experiences, wellness retreats, and yoga classes. Guests can also enjoy healthy cooking classes and explore the resort's beautifully landscaped gardens.

Thailand's wellness retreats and spa resorts provide a sanctuary for travelers seeking to rejuvenate their mind, body, and spirit. The combination of traditional healing practices, tranquil natural settings, and luxurious amenities make Thailand an ideal destination for wellness enthusiasts. Whether indulging in signature spa treatments, practicing mindfulness in serene surroundings, or immersing oneself in healthy cuisine, the diverse offerings of Thai wellness retreats cater to individual preferences and goals. From the serene beaches of Phuket to the cultural richness of Chiang Mai and the lush landscapes of Koh Samui, Thailand offers a myriad of options to embark on a transformative wellness journey.

Travelers seeking ultimate relaxation and holistic well-being will find that Thailand's wellness retreats and spa resorts provide an unparalleled experience, blending ancient wisdom with modern luxury. Immerse yourself in Thailand's rich wellness traditions, let go of stress, and embark on a journey of rejuvenation and self-discovery in the Land of Smiles.

• *Yoga and Meditation Centers*

Open sidebar
Thailand: History & Culture

User
Write about Yoga and Meditation Centers
in Thailand,
in regards to a Thailand travel guide,in 2000
words.

52 / 52

ChatGPT
Title: Exploring Serenity: Yoga and Meditation
Centers in Thailand

Introduction (Word Count: 150)
Thailand, known for its stunning beaches, rich culture, and vibrant street life, has also emerged as a prominent destination for seekers of inner peace and spiritual growth. The

country is home to numerous yoga and meditation centers that offer a sanctuary for individuals to embark on a transformative journey. In this travel guide, we will explore some of the most renowned yoga and meditation centers in Thailand, highlighting their unique offerings, serene locations, and the cultural and natural beauty that surrounds them. Whether you are a beginner or an experienced practitioner, Thailand's yoga and meditation centers provide an ideal setting to nourish your mind, body, and soul.

The Absolute Sanctuary, Koh Samui (Word Count: 350)
Located on the idyllic island of Koh Samui, The Absolute Sanctuary is a haven for yoga and wellness enthusiasts. With its tranquil atmosphere and comprehensive wellness programs, it offers an immersive experience for guests. The center features a wide range of yoga classes, from Hatha to Ashtanga, along with specialized programs such as detox retreats and holistic healing sessions. Accommodations are designed to provide comfort and relaxation, and the resort's spa facilities offer a variety of rejuvenating treatments. Koh Samui's pristine beaches and lush tropical surroundings add to the overall charm of The Absolute Sanctuary.

Tao Garden Health Spa & Resort, Chiang Mai
(Word Count: 400)
Nestled amidst the serene countryside of Chiang Mai, Tao Garden Health Spa & Resort is renowned for its integration of ancient Eastern wisdom with modern wellness practices. This center emphasizes the healing arts of Taoism and offers a wide range of meditation techniques, including Taoist, Buddhist, and Osho meditations. Yoga classes are also available, including Yin Yoga and Qigong. Tao Garden's holistic approach extends to its organic farm, where guests can indulge in nutritious meals made from fresh ingredients. The resort's spacious rooms and rejuvenating spa treatments make for a truly rejuvenating experience.

Kamalaya Wellness Sanctuary, Koh Samui
(Word Count: 400)
Situated amidst the lush vegetation on the southern coast of Koh Samui, Kamalaya Wellness Sanctuary is a renowned destination for those seeking a holistic wellness retreat. The center offers a variety of yoga classes, including Vinyasa and Yin Yoga, as well as meditation sessions and personalized wellness programs. Kamalaya's wellness facilities,

including a herbal steam cavern and plunge pools, provide ample opportunities for relaxation and rejuvenation. The resort's stunning sea views and tranquil ambiance enhance the overall experience, allowing guests to reconnect with nature and find inner balance.

Samahita Retreat, Koh Samui (Word Count Samahita Retreat, located on the pristine beach of Laem Sor, Koh Samui, is a well-established yoga and wellness center. The retreat offers daily yoga classes, ranging from gentle and restorative practices to more dynamic Vinyasa sessions. Meditation sessions and mindfulness practices are also integrated into the retreat's programs. The center's eco-friendly accommodations and delicious vegetarian cuisine contribute to a holistic and sustainable experience. Samahita Retreat's beachfront location offers the perfect backdrop for relaxation and self-reflection, making it an ideal choice for those seeking a peaceful escape.

Museflower Retreat & Spa, Chiang Rai
Nestled in the picturesque countryside of Chiang Rai, Museflower Retreat & Spa is a hidden gem that provides a nurturing

environment for yoga and meditation practitioners. The retreat offers daily yoga classes, including Hatha and Yin Yoga, as well as guided meditation sessions. Additionally, guests can enjoy holistic spa treatments, nature walks, and organic vegetarian meals prepared with locally sourced ingredients. The serene surroundings, including a natural lake and lush gardens, create a peaceful atmosphere that complements the overall wellness experience at Museflower Retreat & Spa.

Thailand's yoga and meditation centers offer a multitude of opportunities for individuals to embark on a journey of self-discovery and inner peace. Whether it's the idyllic beaches of Koh Samui or the serene countryside of Chiang Mai and Chiang Rai, each center provides a unique blend of ancient wisdom, modern wellness practices, and natural beauty. By immersing yourself in the tranquil ambiance and embracing the teachings of yoga and meditation, you can experience a transformative retreat that nurtures both your mind and body. In Thailand's yoga and meditation centers, serenity awaits those who seek it.

CHAPTER TEN

Practical Information

• Packing Tips and What to Bring

Thailand, the land of smiles, is a captivating destination that offers a perfect blend of stunning landscapes, rich cultural heritage, delicious cuisine, and warm hospitality. When planning a trip to Thailand, it is essential to pack wisely to ensure a comfortable and enjoyable experience. In this travel guide, we will provide you with valuable packing tips and a comprehensive list of essential items to bring along on your adventure in Thailand.

I. Weather Considerations:

Thailand experiences a tropical climate, characterized by high temperatures and humidity throughout the year. However, there are variations in weather patterns depending on the region and season. Here are some tips to pack accordingly:

Lightweight Clothing:
Opt for lightweight, breathable fabrics like cotton and linen to combat the heat and humidity. Pack loose-fitting tops, shorts, skirts, and dresses to stay comfortable.

Sun Protection:
Thailand's sun can be intense, so make sure to bring a wide-brimmed hat, sunglasses, and sunscreen with a high SPF. Protecting your skin from the sun is crucial, especially when visiting beach destinations or spending time outdoors.

Rain Gear:
If you're visiting during the rainy season (May to October), pack a lightweight waterproof jacket or poncho. Additionally, carrying a small umbrella is always handy for sudden showers.

II. Essential Items for Exploring Thailand:

Apart from weather-specific items, here are some essential items you should include in your packing list:

Travel Documents:
Passport (with at least six months validity)

Printed copies of your passport, visa, travel insurance, and accommodation bookings

International driving license (if planning to rent a vehicle)

Emergency contact information (family, embassy, travel agent)

Money and Cards:

Thai Baht (THB) and some US dollars for emergencies and currency exchange

Credit/debit cards (inform your bank about your travel plans to avoid any card issues)

Money belt or secure travel wallet for keeping your valuables safe

Travel Electronics:

Universal power adapter (Thailand uses 220V AC electricity with Type A, B, or C sockets)

Mobile phone and charger

Camera or smartphone for capturing memorable moments

Portable power bank for charging on-the-go

Waterproof phone case (for beach activities and water sports)

Medications and Health Essentials:

Prescription medications (in original packaging with a doctor's note if required)

Over-the-counter medications for common ailments like headaches, allergies, and diarrhea

Insect repellent containing DEET

Basic first aid kit with band-aids, antiseptic cream, and any specific personal medications

Travel insurance information and emergency medical contact details

Toiletries and Personal Care Items:

Travel-sized toiletries (shampoo, conditioner, soap, toothpaste, etc.)

Travel towel or quick-dry towel

Hand sanitizer and wet wipes for hygiene purposes

Feminine hygiene products (if required)

Travel-sized laundry detergent (useful for longer trips)

Other Essential Items:

Comfortable walking shoes or sandals

Swimwear and beach towel

Reusable water bottle to stay hydrated (avoid buying single-use plastic bottles)

Travel-sized umbrella for sun and rain protection

Travel pillow and eye mask for long journeys or overnight flights

Lightweight daypack or backpack for day trips and sightseeing

Phrasebook or language translation app to communicate with locals

Thailand offers an array of unforgettable experiences, and proper packing plays a crucial role in making your trip hassle-free and enjoyable. By considering the weather conditions, cultural aspects, and activities you plan to engage in, you can pack smartly for your adventure in Thailand. Remember, packing light and focusing on essentials will give you more flexibility and freedom to explore this beautiful country. So, grab your passport, pack your bags, and get ready to embark on an incredible journey to the Land of Smiles!

•Local Customs and Etiquette

When traveling to Thailand, it is essential to familiarize yourself with the local customs and etiquette to ensure a respectful and enjoyable experience. Thailand is known for its rich cultural heritage, vibrant traditions, and warm hospitality. By understanding and respecting the local customs, you can immerse yourself in the local way of life, connect with the Thai people, and create unforgettable memories. In this Thailand travel guide, we will explore the fascinating customs and etiquette that will enhance your cultural experience in this beautiful Southeast Asian nation.

Greeting and Respect:
Thais value respect and politeness, so it is crucial to greet people properly. The traditional Thai greeting is the "wai," which involves placing your palms together in a prayer-like gesture and bowing slightly. When greeting someone, it is customary to offer a wai and say "Sawasdee" (hello) or "Sawasdee khrap" (hello, if you're male) or "Sawasdee kha" (hello, if you're female). Thais usually use first names, but it's polite to address older individuals with "Khun" followed by their first name.

Clothing and Appearance:
Thailand's climate is generally warm and humid, but it is important to dress modestly, especially when visiting temples or religious sites. Both men and women should avoid wearing revealing clothing or items that expose the shoulders or knees. When entering a temple, it is customary to remove your shoes and dress appropriately. Additionally, the head is considered sacred, so it is respectful to avoid touching people's heads, including children.

Buddhist Customs:

Thailand is a predominantly Buddhist country, and Buddhism heavily influences Thai culture. When visiting temples or religious sites, it is essential to show respect. Dress modestly, speak softly, and refrain from any disrespectful behavior. It is customary to remove your shoes and hat before entering a temple, and avoid pointing your feet towards Buddha images or monks as it is considered impolite. Do not climb or sit on Buddha statues, and if you want to take a photo with a statue, do it respectfully without turning your back towards it.

Thai Cuisine:

Thailand is renowned for its delicious and diverse cuisine. When dining in Thailand, there are a few etiquette guidelines to follow. Thais typically eat with a spoon and fork, using the fork to push food onto the spoon. Chopsticks are primarily used for noodle dishes or Chinese-inspired meals. It is customary to wait for the eldest or the most senior person to start eating before you begin. Additionally, it is polite to try a little of each dish served to you, as it shows appreciation for the host's hospitality.

Tipping and Payments:

Tipping is not traditionally expected in Thailand, but it has become more common in tourist areas. In upscale restaurants, a service charge may be included in the bill. If the service was exceptional, leaving a small tip is appreciated. When paying, hand the money or credit card with both hands as a sign of respect. It is customary to receive the change or receipt with both hands as well.

Public Behavior and Etiquette:
Thais value harmonious interactions and avoiding confrontation. It is important to maintain a calm and friendly demeanor in public. Loud or aggressive behavior is considered impolite. Public displays of affection should be kept to a minimum. Pointing with your finger is considered rude, so it is better to use an open hand or gesture with your chin. When sitting or crossing your legs, avoid pointing your feet at others, as it is seen as disrespectful.

Royalty and National Symbols:
The Thai monarchy is highly respected, and it is important to show reverence to the royal family and national symbols. Criticizing or disrespecting the royal family is a serious offense in Thailand, and it is illegal to deface or

damage Thai currency, which features the king's image. When the Thai national anthem is played, it is customary for everyone to stand still as a sign of respect.

Cultural Sensitivity:
Thailand is a diverse country with various ethnicities and religious beliefs. It is essential to respect and appreciate the cultural diversity you encounter. Avoid discussing sensitive topics such as politics or making derogatory remarks about any religion or culture. Thais are generally welcoming and friendly, so embracing their customs and showing genuine interest will often be met with warmth and appreciation.

By understanding and respecting the local customs and etiquette, your visit to Thailand will be enhanced with authentic cultural experiences and positive interactions with the Thai people. Embrace the warmth and hospitality of this beautiful country, and remember to approach every interaction with kindness, respect, and an open mind. Immerse yourself in Thailand's rich traditions, sample its delicious cuisine, and create lasting memories of this enchanting Southeast Asian destination.

•Emergency Contacts

When traveling to Thailand, it's essential to be well-prepared for any unexpected situations that may arise. One crucial aspect of trip planning is to familiarize yourself with emergency contacts in the country. This comprehensive travel guide aims to provide you with detailed information on emergency services and essential contact numbers in Thailand. By having this knowledge at your fingertips, you can ensure your safety and peace of mind throughout your journey.

General Emergency Services

In case of a life-threatening emergency, the primary number to dial in Thailand is 191. This connects you to the police, who can assist with situations like accidents, crimes, or other emergencies requiring immediate attention. The police hotline is available 24/7 throughout the country.

For medical emergencies, dial 1669 to reach the Thai Red Cross Society's Emergency Medical Service. This service provides ambulance assistance and emergency medical care. Medical facilities in Thailand are generally of good quality, but language barriers can sometimes pose a challenge. It's advisable to keep a list of English-speaking hospitals and clinics in major tourist areas.

Tourist Police

Thailand has a dedicated Tourist Police force that provides assistance specifically for tourists. They are trained to handle tourist-related matters, such as lost passports, theft, or scams. The Tourist Police can be reached by dialing 1155 from anywhere in Thailand. They operate 24/7 and have English-speaking officers to help international visitors.

Embassy and Consular Contacts

In the event of a serious emergency or if you require assistance from your country's diplomatic mission, it's crucial to have the contact information of your embassy or consulate. Here are some key embassy contact details in Thailand:

United States Embassy:

Address: 120-122 Wireless Road, Bangkok
Phone: +66 (0)2 205 4000
After-hours Emergency: +66 (0)2 205 4000
British Embassy:

Address: 14 Wireless Road, Lumpini, Pathumwan, Bangkok
Phone: +66 (0)2 305 8333
After-hours Emergency: +66 (0)2 305 8333
Australian Embassy:

Address: 181 Wireless Road, Lumpini, Pathumwan, Bangkok
Phone: +66 (0)2 344 6300
After-hours Emergency: +61 2 6261 3305
It's recommended to register your travel plans with your embassy or consulate before arriving in Thailand. This facilitates easy communication in case of emergencies or important updates from your home country.

Local Emergency Services (300 words)
Apart from general emergency numbers, Thailand has specific hotlines for various services:

Fire Department: 199

Tourist Service Center: 1672
Highway Police: 1193
Marine Police: 1196
Anti-Human Trafficking Hotline: 1300
Useful Mobile Apps (200 words)
Several mobile apps can assist you in emergencies and provide additional safety measures while in Thailand:

Tourist Buddy: Developed by the Tourism Authority of Thailand, this app provides essential travel information, safety tips, emergency contacts, and real-time alerts.

LINE MAN: A popular delivery app in Thailand that offers a "Help Now" feature in case of emergencies. It allows you to connect with emergency services or call for assistance.

By familiarizing yourself with emergency contacts in Thailand, you can ensure a safe and secure trip. Whether you need assistance from the police, medical services, or your embassy, knowing the relevant contact numbers is essential. Additionally, understanding the role of the Tourist Police and utilizing helpful mobile apps can further enhance your safety and overall travel experience.

Remember, emergencies can happen anywhere, and being prepared with the right information can make a significant difference. Always keep important contact numbers accessible, share your travel plans with someone back home, and exercise caution while exploring Thailand. With proper planning and awareness, you can enjoy your trip while feeling confident that you are well-equipped to handle any unforeseen circumstances.

CHAPTER ELEVEN

Conclusion and Final Tips

In conclusion, Thailand is a captivating destination that offers a perfect blend of natural beauty, rich cultural heritage, vibrant cities, and warm hospitality. This travel guide has aimed to provide comprehensive information and insights to help you plan a memorable trip to Thailand. From the bustling streets of Bangkok to the serene beaches of Phuket, this country offers something for every type of traveler.

One of the most important aspects of traveling to Thailand is to respect the local customs and traditions. Thais are known for their friendliness and politeness, and by showing respect and understanding, you can create positive interactions and memorable experiences. Additionally, being aware of cultural norms such as dressing modestly when visiting temples and removing your shoes before entering someone's home or a sacred space is crucial.

Thailand's cuisine is renowned worldwide, and trying the local food is a must-do when visiting the country. From the vibrant flavors of street food to the delicate dishes served in high-end restaurants, Thai cuisine is a sensory delight. Don't be afraid to explore the local markets and sample dishes like pad Thai, green curry, and mango sticky rice.

Transportation in Thailand is relatively efficient, with options like trains, buses, and tuk-tuks readily available. However, be prepared for traffic congestion in major cities, especially during peak hours. Planning your itinerary in advance and allowing for extra travel time will help you make the most of your trip.

Thailand's natural beauty is unparalleled, with stunning islands, national parks, and mountains waiting to be explored. Whether you're diving in the crystal-clear waters of the Andaman Sea, trekking through the lush jungles of Chiang Mai, or relaxing on the pristine beaches of Krabi, make sure to take time to immerse yourself in the natural wonders of the country.

While Thailand is generally a safe country for travelers, it's always wise to take precautions. Be mindful of your belongings, especially in crowded areas, and avoid carrying large sums of cash or valuable items. Stay hydrated, wear sunscreen, and protect yourself against mosquito bites, especially in areas where malaria and dengue fever are prevalent.

Lastly, don't limit yourself to the popular tourist destinations. Thailand has numerous off-the-beaten-path gems that are waiting to be discovered. Consider exploring the northern provinces of Chiang Rai and Nan, where you'll find ancient temples, lush landscapes, and a slower pace of life. Alternatively, head to the northeastern region of Isaan for a taste of authentic Thai culture and rural charm.

In summary, a trip to Thailand promises an unforgettable experience filled with vibrant culture, stunning landscapes, mouthwatering cuisine, and warm-hearted people. By following this travel guide and embracing the essence of Thailand, you'll create lifelong memories and gain a deeper appreciation for this remarkable country. So pack your bags, embark on an adventure, and get ready to be enchanted by the Land of Smiles.

Final Tips:

Respect the local customs and traditions.
Try the diverse and delicious Thai cuisine.
Plan your transportation and consider traffic congestion.
Immerse yourself in Thailand's natural beauty.
Take precautions to ensure your safety.
Explore off-the-beaten-path destinations for unique experiences.
Embrace the essence of Thailand and its warm-hearted people.
Remember, traveling is about immersing yourself in new cultures, embracing differences, and creating memories. Enjoy your journey to Thailand and embrace the magic that awaits you in the Land of Smiles!